COLLABORATION FOR AUTHORS

A COMPLETE GUIDE TO COLLABORATING,
FINDING A PARTNER, AND ACCELERATING
YOUR AUTHOR CAREER.

DANIEL WILLCOCKS

PRESS

OTHER TITLES BY DANIEL WILLCOCKS

The Rot Series (with Luke Kondor)

They Rot (Book 1)

They Remain (Book 2)

They Ruin (coming soon)

Keep My Bones

The Caitlin Chronicles (with Michael Anderle)

(1) Dawn of Chaos

(2) Into the Fire

(3) Hunting the Broken

(4) The City Revolts

(5) Chasing the Cure

Other Works

Twisted: A Collection of Dark Tales

Lazarus: Enter the Deadspace

The Mark of the Damned

Sins of Smoke

Keep up-to-date at

www.danielwillcocks.com

A SPECIAL THANKS TO MY PATRONS

To every single patron that supports the Great Writers Share podcast, and all the work that I put in behind the scenes, this one is for you.

Jenn Mitchell
Michael Anderle
Yanni Jade
Mark M
Ian J Middleton
Harley Christensen
Dave
Katie Forrest
P.T. Hylton
Innes Richens
Jon Cronshaw
Meg Cowley

*Want **your** name featured in future Great Writers Share series books? Then head over to www.patreon.com/greatwritersshare and get involved! Subscriptions start from just $1 a month.*

CONTENTS

Foreword   xi
Introduction   xiii

PART I
1. Collaboration expectations vs reality   3

PART II
2. Is collaboration right for you?   11
2.1. Leave your ego at the door   13
2.2. Honesty is the only policy   16
2.3. Knowing your worth   19
2.4. Accountability   25
2.5. Control freaks   28
2.6. Trust   31
2.7. Meet your new spouse   33
2.8. Building a track record   36
2.9. "No"   39
2.10. The collaboration equation   42
2.11. Expert panel   45
2.12. Summary   47

Collaboration Case Study: J. Thorn and Zach   50
Bohannon

PART III
3. Types of collaboration   61
3.1. Co-writing   63
3.1.1. One-offs   65
3.1.2. Sharing your own universe   68
3.1.3. Playing in someone else's sandpit   72
3.2. Publishing partnerships   75
3.3. Ghostwriting   79
3.4 Accountability partners   85

3.5. Ideation 88
3.6. Anthologies and box sets 91
3.7. The melting pot of collaboration 95
3.8. Summary 97

Collaboration Case Study: Angeline Trevena and 100
H.B. Lyne

PART IV
4. Finding your collaborator 109
4.1. Identify what you can bring to the table 111
4.2. The wrong way 115
4.3. The right way 119
4.4. After you click send 128
4.5. After the yes 130
4.6. Summary 132

Collaboration Case Study: Michael Anderle 134

PART V
5. Laying the foundations 141
5.1. (Dis)Agreements 143
5.2. The (dis)agreement checklist 146
5.3. Collaboration red flags 155
5.4. Summary 164

Collaboration Case Study: Kathrin Hutson 166

PART VI
6. Getting stuck in 175
6.1. Ideation and story 177
6.2. Marketing and planning 185
6.3. Publication 196
6.4. Financial tracking 202
6.5. Summary 207

Collaboration Case Study: LE Barbant 210

PART VII

7. When collaborations go wrong   219

PART VIII
8. Expert panel: Final words from the pros   227

Go forth, young collaborator   230
Thanks (and bonus content)   233
Expert panel members   235
Acknowledgments   239
About the Author   241

APPENDIX
How I'm co-writing two novels with @lukeofkondor   247
Writing with the enemy   252

Continue Your Collaboration Journey   259
Other titles by Daniel Willcocks   261

FOREWORD

I first met Daniel Willcocks while listening to "The Other Stories" podcast, and I knew right away that he was a thoughtful, articulate, and intelligent guy. It takes a massive amount of coordination and collaboration to produce a podcast of that magnitude. And I should know, given that I've co-written with dozens of people and produced more than 500 podcast episodes over the past six years.

But I've also had the pleasure of collaborating with Dan in my *American Demon Hunters* series, and that's when I observed his dedication to the craft of writing and his ability to collaborate, even from across the Atlantic Ocean. Dan approached our project with commitment and professionalism, not something to be assumed in any collaborative effort.

When Dan asked to interview me (along with my business partner, Zach Bohannon) for this book, I knew I couldn't resist the opportunity to provide additional insight for those considering a collaboration. Let's be honest. Collaboration can be a frustrating experience, and yet it can also be the most gratifying aspect of any creative endeavour—and those feelings can exist within the same project.

You're in for an entertaining and informative ride. Dan has spent the better part of five years collaborating and co-writing with many people. He's learned what works and what doesn't, and he generously shares that advice in this book. Dan identifies and walks you through the process of collaboration, and more importantly, shows you the potential pitfalls. He taps other friends in the industry, providing a well-rounded and broad sampling of how authors are co-writing.

Discover if collaboration is right for you and if it is, why you need to leave your ego at the door. Learn how to hold your partner (and yourself) accountable for the work. Although you might not know it, your collaborator is like a spouse.

Dan's sense of humour and good nature shines through even when he's talking about legal (dis)agreements as well as red flags that might help you avoid a collaboration calamity.

The book in your hand is a light-hearted and yet deep dive into what it takes to be a collaborator. There isn't a more qualified writer to tackle this topic, and I know you'll learn from Dan, just as I have.

J. Thorn
theauthorlife.com
May 2020

INTRODUCTION

Collaboration.

It's the buzzword of the hour, a word very much in vogue, and yet little has been done or said to explore just what exactly all of the fuss is about.

We see the boasts and the celebrations in the forums, we see writers chaining their arms in union and publishing several books a month, we hear about success stories on the daily, and we wish we had someone with whom we could collaborate.

Who wouldn't want a work-wife/husband who could make all of our efforts that little bit easier, and give us a friendly shoulder to lean on? Someone to lessen the load and join us on this stony path we call writing? Someone who can hold our fingers to the fire and scream in our faces until the work is done...

But I digress. Before we get ahead of ourselves too much, we should probably ask ourselves:

What exactly is collaboration?

Collaboration is a malleable process. It's almost impossible to define just what exactly is meant by the term as, in most cases, collaborations are incredibly unique and brilliant. I should know. I've had a number of collaborations for nearly half a decade, partnering with writers and creatives across a number of written productions and podcasts, and yet not one of the damn things has been in any way uniform or cookie-cut.

We think of collaborations and there's almost a fantasy veil that glosses our eyes. We think of webcam business meetings (in our pants), we imagine being able to create order from the chaos of our splatter box minds, and we think about buddying up with our peers and making a real go of this shitshow that we call writing.

But to those of you who have yet to cross over to the dark side and bond with your creative brothers and sisters-in-arms, it's worth considering:

What are collaborations really like?

That's the question that I'm here to answer for you. As one great writing podcast states in its upbeat intro: "It's no secret that writing can be lonely work, but does it really have to be?" (For those of you wondering, yes, that's from my own podcast, "Great Writers Share". You think I'm going to write a non-fiction book for authors, and not share the news?) And it's true. Collaborations can bring out the best in us. They can cut through the sticky viscous layer of self-doubt and imposter syndrome that descends upon us when we're in our offices writing alone and make us feel somewhat connected to other human beings. They can be glorious, and enlightening, and motivating, and empowering, and help you accelerate to the next level in your author career.

Yet, for some, collaborations can also be crippling and suffocating and exacerbate all of your worries and fears about yourself and your credibility as a writer. They can end in fallouts, broken friendships, and even lead you down that narrow road towards packing it all in and thinking that you'll never make it in this profession.

I'd like to help you with all of that. I'd like to act as something of a Jiminy Cricket, standing on your shoulder and whispering sweet guidance in your ear. I'd like to give you as much knowledge as I've learned while navigating the minefield of collaborations. I want to help you set off with your best foot forward and find the path that truly works for you (there are a thousand paths ahead, after all).

"But, Dan!" I hear you cry, knowing that I prefer Dan to Daniel among my friends (and we're all friends, here). "Who the hell are you to give us advice?" And it's a fair question.

Meet your mentor

I'm Daniel Willcocks, internationally best-selling author of dark fiction.

My journey with collaborations began very early on in my writing career. After publishing my first solo novella in 2015, I joined with a fledgling story studio alongside three other dudes and we started working together to publish horror, sci-fi, and thriller fiction under the company name of "Hawk & Cleaver".

There are a whole host of podcasts episodes on the World Wide Web where I talk about the inception of Hawk & Cleaver, so I won't go into the nitty-gritty, here. Suffice to say that by publishing both fiction podcasts and non-fiction podcasts, I ended up on a journey in which I reached out to other authors and joined alongside some of the biggest names currently in independent fiction. The rest, as they say, is ~~misery~~ history.

In my five years of working (and playing) with creatives across all mediums, I've successfully published over 1.5 million words of fiction across a range of genres and pen names. Many of those have been best-sellers, though some have been flops. I've also played a large part in publishing over 200+ episodes of podcasted fiction, alongside my Hawk & Cleaver brothers at "The Other Stories" podcast, which has been downloaded over 5 million times, as at the time of publication of this book.

I've played with ghostwriting, I've written in people's worlds, I've co-written in 50:50 relationships, and I've learned a thing or two about how to collaborate, who to collaborate with, and how to make it work.

Shall we agree that you're in good hands? Okay, then. Let us proceed.

What will this book teach you?

This book is going to act as your manual to collaborations. A "Collaboration 101", if you will. In the pages ahead, I'll lay the foundations of:

- Who collaboration is (and isn't) for
- Moulding your mindset to work with others
- The main types of collaboration, and the pros and cons of each
- How to approach potential collaborators and optimize your first impressions for maximum success
- The intricacies of working with other collaborators
- Protecting yourself and your intellectual property (IP) with solid agreements
- Collaboration red flags

- Specific tools you may find useful when collaborating
- How to deal with collaborations if (and when) they go wrong

Along the way, you'll be introduced to some of the biggest names in the fiction collaboration sphere. I've injected this book with real-world examples, opinions, and advice from a panel of experts among all types of collaboration; from those who have created multi-million selling fictional universes, to ghostwriters, to accountability partners, and those who flourish by writing in the imaginations of others.

I've even included a full essay contribution by an author friend who was burned by a previous collaboration—so that you can see both sides of the coin and try to learn from the mistakes of those who have gone before you—as well as the original full blog post that details my first ever experimental collaboration with co-author, Luke Kondor. This book is not a rose-tinted view on collaboration, and you will see both ends of the spectrum. Collaboration is a wild game of chance, but there's a lot you can do to increase your odds of success.

If I've done my job right, by the end of this book you'll be sufficiently clued up on everything you need to know to get started on your journey, and have a smooth collaboration, if that is the path you wish to choose.

One final note

This is not a book about the finer points of legality and finance. While I recommend services and processes to handle these facets, if you are looking to understand the full logistics of managing finances within your author career, or the perfect contract to secure your business dealings with your collaborator, then this is not the book for you.

I will load your wagon full of knowledge rocks and kick it down the hill for you.

The journey is yours.

However, be warned: you best keep up. Once gravity gets a hold of that wagon and gets it rolling, you've got a hell of a ride ahead.

So, strap in.

PART I

COLLABORATION EXPECTATIONS VS REALITY

1. COLLABORATION EXPECTATIONS VS REALITY

B efore we chomp into the juicy flesh of this collaboration melon, I thought it best to look at debunking some of the common myths associated with collaborating, as well as laying out some truth bombs of what to expect when you're looking at collaborations.

Expectation is fundamentally key to collaborations (as we'll come onto later), so before we step into the collaborena, here are some of the most common myths and beliefs, and the truth that lies beneath. You'll notice that some of these myths explore the positive outcomes of collaboration, while others look at the negatives. There are always two sides to a coin, folks. At least on this planet, anyway.

Myth 1. It'll be so easy!

This is one of the largest myths out there. Sure, collaborations have the *potential* to be simple, and to make your life easier, but the truth *can* be far from it. Michael Anderle, CEO of LMPBN Publishing and creator of the best-selling *Kurtherian Gambit* universe, notes, "[People think] it's going to be rainbows and unicorns, or something along those lines. Collaborations can be a lot of fun, but stress-free (or ego-free) is usually not one of them."

In fact, often, it can actually be more complicated than writing solo. Depending on how you approach your collaboration, you may find it accommodates more head space than if you work alone. "It's harder and there are strengths and weaknesses to the collaboration," says Nick Cole, Dragon Award-winning author and co-creator of the *Galaxy's Edge* series.

So, wipe away that preconception that it's going to be smooth sailing. While that *can* be the case, more often than not, it's just a different kind of work—one that yields its own unique set of rewards.

Myth 2. Collaborating is faster than writing my own work and will increase my output

Ramy Vance, best-selling author of urban fantasy, and creator of the *GoneGod World* sums it up best: "I have collaborated with five authors. In two cases, it meant faster production, but in three it actually slowed things down."

It's all a game of give and take. Collaborating *can* make your output faster, but again it's like sticking your hand in a bag of nails and hoping that you pull out the chocolate bar. If you're planning on collaborating a lot, then you may find that any speed increase you had with your first projects balance out as others slow you down.

In my first collaboration, it wasn't the physical act of collaborating that sped me and my co-writer up—it was the accountability we shared and being held responsible for various jobs. It could have been possible to write the books by myself in the same amount of time, though at the time I didn't entirely know it.

Myth 3. Collaboration will sky-rocket my success

Unless you're collaborating with James Patterson, you should probably kick this idea out of your head straight away.

Collaboration is no different to writing solo, in this regard. The quality of your product and the marketing efforts you put into your sales are what will determine your book's success and, consequently, your success as an author. While two heads can be better than one, and you may experience minor boosts along the way, it's very rare that a collaboration will chokeslam you straight into the big leagues.

Myth 4. Collaborating with friends is a bad idea

While I *have* seen collaborations which have destroyed friendships, as well as collaborations which have turned friends into *best* friends (and, in some cases, romantic couples), they don't always have to be so dichotomous in the final outcome. According to author of dark fiction author, and co-host of the *Unstoppable Authors* podcast, Angeline Trevena, "It's not a case that, if you collaborate on a project, you'll either never speak again or your future collaborations will be perfect. There's no perfect relationship, and they change day by day. Switching to becoming partners on a work project will change aspects of your friendship, but it doesn't rewrite the whole thing. It's merely one part of your ongoing, ever-changing relationship."

As we'll go on to explore, the outcome of your collaboration will depend entirely on how you approach your collaboration from start to finish. There are absolutely right ways and wrong ways to collaborate, but it doesn't always have to end up in such dichotomous straits.

Myth 5. Collaborating improves the quality of the work

This is asking Aunt Sarah to hook you up with an artist to paint you a replica of Leonardo da Vinci's "Mona Lisa". You just won't know until they invite you around for the grand reveal and either show you a perfect copy of that beautiful Lisa dame, or reveal a clumsy image of a deep-battered hag which looked like it may have been fished out from the bottom of the riverbed.

You don't know until you know. If you can play nicely and take each other's criticism, and both commit to making a product that's the best it can be, then maybe you have a hope. It's not a guarantee, but it definitely elevates those odds. Best-selling author, podcaster, and co-owner of Molten Universe Media, Zach Bohannon, says, "It's a different kind of work. I think it makes it better, but it's not easier."

Myth 6. Your creative freedom is stifled when collaborating

This can be a mixed bag and, like all of the other points we've listed above, depend entirely on your collaboration.

Creativity is different in collaborations. You're now in a situation where someone can "Veto" an idea if they don't like it. What this brings is new challenges, new ways to stimulate your creativity. You flex muscles you've never had to flex before because you've had no one testing the strength of your ideas before you start work on them.

In my experience, I've been creatively satisfied in most of my endeavours. If anything, it can be fun to try and find the best ways to blend and mesh your uniqueness with your collaborators. It makes for a fun reader experience. "You have to be willing to compromise," says Craig Martelle, best-selling science-fiction author.

There can also be fears that you're "selling your soul", or that you're going to "lose your voice", and that's not always true. Some of my collaborative works reflect my voice better than some of my individual works and, as for selling out, just consider what your end goal is and how you want to get there. No one way is the "right" way.

Myth 7. Readers won't follow you from a collaborative work to your own individual body of work

This one can be really hit and miss, but there is a kernel of truth in there. For the most part, if you're creating good quality works, and you're pleasing the fans enough with what you're doing, then there's nothing to stop them diving into your backlist and checking out the goods.

However, conversion rates depend on the project. If you're usually a writer of space opera, and you collaborate on a cosy mystery, you can bet your bottom dollar that readers are probably not going to trailblaze through the cosmos and jump about the DX-93 en route to Kahligznam (if you're a writer of space opera, forgive me, I know that was terrible).

But if you are collaborating with an author who is already in the same genre as yourself and you write a book that links very nicely with your backlist, collaboration can be a great way to introduce yourself to a whole host of rabid, hungry readers.

Myth 8. There's only one way to collaborate

Sigh

I hear this one a lot, and for the purposes of giving some kind of answer, I'll keep this one simple.

Thinking that there's only one way to collaborate is the same as saying there's only one flavour of ice-cream. It's the same as saying there's only one way to tie a knot. It's the same as thinking that there's a right way to succeed in authorship.

In short, it's just BS.

WHILE THIS LIST of expectations is by no means extensive, it certainly covers the main whispers I hear on the wind. For those who haven't collaborated before, it can be intimidating, and you need to know what you're in for before you get started.

Luckily for you, the next chapter will start you along your guided collaboration tour.

PART II

IS COLLABORATION RIGHT FOR YOU?

2. IS COLLABORATION RIGHT FOR YOU?

This is a pretty big question, and you may or may not already have the answer in your mind. Let me hurl a knowledge bomb at your face:

Collaboration isn't for everyone.

That's the cold, hard truth. In the same way that only a select portion of the population prefer dogs over cats, and an even smaller majority of the elderly like to yell at wheelie bins for loitering down their streets, collaborations may not suit everyone's personality type.

Sure, you may be sitting there and thinking, "But, Dan, what's the point in me picking up this book if you're going to tell me I shouldn't collaborate?" And you'd be well within your right to ask such a thing. So, in response, I'd like to ask you a question...

Why do *you* want to collaborate?

We've already gone through some of the key myths around collaboration, but this is one of the key questions you're going to want to ask yourself, first.

- Are you looking to collaborate because you're trying to take shortcuts?
- Are you aiming to use someone's success as a steppingstone for your own? (Not a judgement, I've done this on a few occasions, ensuring that the agreement was mutually beneficial—more on that later).
- Are you trying to become less of a control freak and get over your innate desire to make every last word perfect on the page?
- Are you hoping to learn the ways of craft from writers who are several steps ahead of you on their journey?

Whatever your reason for collaborating is, there are only a handful of things that are going to help determine whether or not you have what it takes to make this work.

Luckily for you, I've put these into a handy, easy-to-digest summary in the sections ahead.

2.1. LEAVE YOUR EGO AT THE DOOR

Collaborations should *never* be about ego. Collaborations create a product greater than the sum of its parts, and it takes many hands on the wheel in order to guide this freight-liner along its merry voyage.

Ego is something that every writer begins with, at least in my experience. Every writer wants to craft the "next great [insert country here] novel" and see their names at the No. 1 spot of the charts. Of course, you do. You want to be lauded for your work. You want validation from peers and strangers that you have the God-given talent to be a writer. You want the money to roll in and for the world to become your clam... oyster... some kind of shellfish.

The reality of writing is vastly different to the expectations of the newbie writer or the starving artist. To become successful in this game it takes one of two things:

1. A lightning strike, captured in a bottle, published by Harper Collins, and broadcast on Prime Time TV.
2. Relentless hard work, a continual shoving of a

boulder up a hill, and delivering quality content to
your readers on a consistent basis.

Sure, you may just be the next J.K. Rowling or Josh
Malerman of this generation, waiting to be discovered but
remember that even those guys had a number of rejections and
less successful books behind them.

**Ego gets you nowhere, whether you choose to go solo, or you
choose to collaborate.**

So, check that shit at the door before you even think of dragging another writer into this madness.

This is one of the first things I address in *every* collaboration
I pursue. Before I've even broached the subject with the desired
collaborator, I have a personal conversation with the devils on
my shoulder (my angel died long ago) and try to understand my
motives for why I'm getting involved in a project. I've got enough
collaborations behind me to know that *I* can leave my ego at the
door, but there's always the question of: *can they?*

Collaborating is a two-person (or more) effort—*duh!* The
product that *you're* imagining is likely to be vastly different to
the product that you will make together. You will both have
ideas that you love, and you will both have ideas that you hate.
You will have to learn when to enact the power of "veto", and
you'll need to know where the boundaries lay.

The reality is that collaborations can be hard work, and at
the end of the day, you still need to be able to hold up your
finished novel, non-fic, anthology—whatever you create—with
pride. It's likely going to have your name on it. Can you honestly
say that it will represent you and your brand in the best possible
light?

If the answer to this question is "yes," then you're ready to continue to the next phase. If the answer is "no," or "not sure," then spend some time to think about why *you* are thinking of collaborating, and whether you can put your ego aside, and focus on the larger goal.

When asked what situations have put some of his collaborations in jeopardy, Michael Anderle says, "The ones that stick out are when two collaborators are very opinionated. Usually, it can be from those who have less experience wanting exactly what they would do if they were solo." If you are unwilling to accept that a collaboration will be a whole new ball game from writing individually, ask yourself if this is for you.

There's no pressure here. Be honest with yourself. In my experience, lying to yourself and forcing something that isn't true to your personality or goals will eventually surface in the collaboration. Like a kid pooping in a public swimming pool, it may be quiet and undetectable at first, but eventually someone will notice, and everyone involved will be left in tears.

2.2. HONESTY IS THE ONLY POLICY

We've heard it a thousand times before. The old mantra your mother used to tell you to stop you stealing gum from the store. Not that it always worked (sorry, Chris, I had to tell someone sometime, the guilt has been on my conscience for far too long). Honesty is the best policy.

As we grow up and become tangled in our own versions of the truth, we can sometimes get into the habit of shrouding ourselves in white lies. We tell our friends we're fine when we're hurting inside. We promise ourselves we'll hit the gym three times a week and stare at our beer guts in shame. We say we'll call our parents when we get time, but life takes precedence and sweeps us away.

"What does this have to do with collaborations," you may be thinking. "Well, give me a second, I'm getting to it," I'll reply.

When you're collaborating, you're dealing with human beings. We humans are marvellous biological machines capable of incredible feats of multi-taskery and skill. Humans have collaboratively created cities, found cures for incurable diseases, and even put a man on the goddamn moon (if you're a true believer, #ArmstrongFTW1969).

But we can also be flaky and vulnerable and unreliable at times. As amazing and as capable as we are of soaring close to the sun, sometimes we plummet into the sea. When collaborations go right, they're great for this sort of thing. Collaborators can catch us before we turn into flesh-squash. They can hold our hands and guide us through the tough times. They give us a chance to help others and unite along this path we call life.

A rising tide raises all ships.

The greatest collaborations are the ones where we're direct and true. Being open, honest, and transparent gives both of you the clarity you need to succeed and opens you up to a support system unlike any you've known before. Between you both, you can celebrate the wins with even more levity. Between you both, you can pound those noggins together and create something beautiful. Between you both, you can transcend the writing arena, and create some of the strongest relationships you've ever known.

> "Whenever I hit potholes in the collaborative road (and while those are few and far between now, I'd be lying if I said I didn't come across my fair share of them starting out), I go immediately for honesty and opening up a space on my end for my collaborators and I to discuss what went wrong and how we can improve."
>
> — KATHRIN HUTSON

There is no one right way to collaborate, in the same way that no two people are the same. You may have an off day. You may have promised your collaborator you'd get the draft to them by Friday, but something unexpected has come along. Illness, childcare, family deaths, the taxman, no matter what it is, you have to be willing to be upfront and let your collaborator know what's going on. And it works both ways. You need to be confident that your collaborator will be honest with you, too. No collaboration is wholly one-sided.

Being honest gives you permission to succeed, but it also gives you permission to fail.

There's little worse than being in the dark about a real issue that a collaborator feels they can't share, but directly impacts both of your work. In the same way that there's not much worse than knowing that you are privy to knowledge that will directly affect your collaborator and choosing to keep it to yourself.

Withheld information is a tapeworm. It'll eat away at you until it finds its own way to purge itself from your body.

The truth will eventually prevail, and it's up to you to decide whether it's from a position of honesty, or a position of deceit.

There have been times in my own collaborations where I've been unable to meet deadlines and times when a project has failed. Being honest gives you both permission to fail because sometimes collaborations don't work out. Sometimes things change. There's no point flogging a dead horse. Your time is precious. Use it wisely on the things that are right for *you* and your career.

2.3. KNOWING YOUR WORTH

If you're reading this book (and I'm pretty confident that you are), then I'm going to make an assumption, here.

You are serious about your author career. You are ready to take the next steps to level up and create some beautiful content to feed the millions of baby-bird-mouthed-readers hovering in the digisphere.

You are a writer. Whether you're traditionally published, or hybrid, or self-published, or haven't even put a fat fleshy digit to the keyboard, you are a writer.

That's a hard one for people to digest, as I personally know that a large part of the beginning of any writing career is knowing *when* to call yourself a writer—as if you need permission. Well, let me give it to you now, fellow writer. Jump in this metal bathtub and join your brothers and sisters in the suds.

You. Are. A. Writer.

That means you have goals. That means you have hopes and dreams. That means you have a favourite genre. That means you have a preferred writing style. That means that you write at a certain time of day. That means that you write for a certain type of audience. That means that you're willing to put in the time to create quality content to deliver to readers the world over.

You stand for something. You may not be sure what that thing is yet, but my guess is that you have some direction, or at least some inkling of a thought. In my early writer days, I dived straight into the world of horror novellas. One year later I was writing post-apocalyptic books. The next year I was writing dark paranormal science-fiction. Now I'm back to writing horror. Delicious, dark, flesh-eating, zombie-staggering, rip-your-heart-out-horror.

And I friggin' love it.

Things change over time, but your core values don't.

All of my fiction contains the thread of the stories I want to tell. They contain relatable characters, they delve deep into the human psyche, and they feature some kind of paranormal or occult horror, demon, or creature.

This is something I stand by. I write a certain type of story, and they're the ones I want connected publicly with my name. (I also ghostwrite alternative fiction under a pen name, but we'll cover that later.) That means that, whenever I look at a possible collaboration, there's a certain type of person that I'm looking for.

It's easy for people to take advantage of the idea of collaboration. It seems like a great idea to partner with someone who can write 10,000 words a day and deliver you first drafts every couple of weeks so all you have to do is edit. It seems even greater having a team of people delivering work for you in a way that means you get to take all the credit for the successes.

But in every collaboration, there needs to be a balance.

Let's call this idea the "Collaboration Scales". In a perfect world, all collaborations would be equal. Both parties benefit. 50:50. An equal split.

The scales of collaboration (50:50)

Yet the truth is often far from that. I think the closest I've ever come to a 50:50 split is my first collaborations, in which I paired with award-winning filmmaker, comic book creator, and fellow Hawk & Cleaver founder, Luke Kondor.

When I first approached the idea of co-writing with Luke, he already had awards under his name. He was already crafting his first comic book. He had already proven he could create fantastic short stories (I'm not kidding, that guy leaves me drooling with envy), and he also had two novels to his name.

I had a single novella, and a handful of short stories.

The great thing about working with Luke was that every conversation we had felt like we were on a level playing field. We checked our ego at the door, and we were honest and upfront about what *we both wanted* from the collaboration (see "4. Laying the foundations"). Yet, even then, a part of me knew that I had more to gain from writing with his name, than he did from mine (even if he might not totally see it that way—humble toe-rag).

Therefore, my first collaboration, as even as it seemed on the surface, was probably more along the lines of the below. The lower the scale, the more likely someone is to benefit from the outcome.

The scales of collaboration (45:55)

And then there's the other side of the scales. Maybe you get lucky enough to work with someone who already has an established universe and readership. Maybe you find that you've won the lottery, and suddenly you're picked up by the indie author equivalent of Stephen King.

Now you're in a position in which you are definitely going to be getting more from the collaboration than your partner is.

These types of collaborations can tip the scales almost entirely. Though, again, the surface value may show something else entirely to the truth that lies underneath.

Say you are one of the lucky ones, and you do find yourself in a collaboration that will accelerate your author career. Maybe a six-figure author has taken a chance on you, a relatively unknown author, and you have the opportunity to start writing full time and crafting the stories that you love.

For a collaboration like this, you'll likely have to do the heavy lifting. Perhaps your collaborator wants you to write all the words and craft the story on their behalf, but they're willing to split royalties and stick your name on the cover. Maybe all they have to do is keep an overview on your story and let their team take care of the work. When it comes to manpower hours, you're definitely in with the lion's share.

In that case, the scales would likely look like this.

The scales of collaboration (20:80)

Each variation of the scales serves to show a different weight on each collaboration, but the truth is that with greater input, comes greater reward.

In the first example, Luke and I ended up crafting three novels which we are incredibly proud of and helped us build our backlists at a faster rate than we would otherwise have been able to ourselves. I think it's safe to say we both benefited equally from that.

In the above example, it may seem on the surface that you are putting in a greater amount of work, yet the balance restores itself in that you gain double the rewards for your efforts. Maybe you spend 60 hours writing the book, but you also benefit from the promotion of your name in its association with an established author (and the royalties may not be that bad, too).

X% contribution = X% rewards

All of this is to say that, no matter how much you think you're contributing to a project, you have your own values and you should know your worth. If the opportunity is right, someone needs your skills. There may be a collaborator out there in need of someone just like you, and it's important that you don't get swindled or tricked into thinking that you're in for a great deal when you're not.

Have you released 10 books in your own name? Then great! You are a published author with a reliable track record. That counts for something.

Are you a fledgling writer who's looking for their first foray into novelling? Super! Find someone who needs a rosy-cheeked junior who's willing to put in the hard work to help.

But, whatever you do, don't jump into a collaboration because you think you *should*. Look at the terms of your agreement and understand where *you* are on your journey and what you are *truly* worth to your potential collaborator.

My bet is that you're definitely worth more than you think.

2.4. ACCOUNTABILITY

Accountability can be a red word for some people. For many, making yourself accountable can either be the greatest gift in the world or a fearsome curse.

We want to write. We want to write at our own pace. We want to deliver our own work when we want to. We want to work on our own terms and not give a damn what you, Doug, Mum, or anyone says!

Ah, the human is a flawed creature.

As alluded to earlier, humans always have the best of intentions, yet when left to our own devices, we find better, easier ways to entertain ourselves.

Netflix is a thing.

Video gaming is cheap and easily accessible.

Sometimes baking is more fun than laboriously pulling at your hair and trying to find the perfect synonym to replace "incredibly" because you've already used it four times in one paragraph.

Our lizard brains don't want us to write. They don't want us to stare at a screen for an hour and hammer at the keyboard. They want us to find quick fixes to pleasure. They want us to eat, sleep, fart, procreate, and do literally anything that will stand in the way of our productivity until we've got no choice left but to crumble and fall.

Mmm crumble...

Stephen Pressfield describes it best in his book, *The War of Art*. He coins this oppressive, distracting force "Resistance". A power that is inbuilt from years of biological programming that systemically drags you away from doing the work that matters.

There's a reason Auntie Sandrine has a hundred forgotten chalk paintings in her garage.

There's a story behind Papa Elton's stacks of half-finished musical scores rotting in the damp attic.

The truth of the author life is that writing is *fucking* hard. Many of us barely win the fight against ourselves, so throwing another person into the equation can appear debilitating. You may say to yourself, "I can't even hit my own deadlines, how can I meet someone else's? What if I let them down?"

Alas, there is hope, dear writer.

For those among us who have collaborated, the reality is very different to the fable. While you may think you need some space to figure out your writing schedule, re-plan your work for the next three months for the fifth time in a week, and browse online for the latest project diary, having a collaborator injects a secret special juice that kicks you up the ass and drives you into a gear that you didn't know you had.

Writing is all about momentum, ask anyone. One month you're writing 50 words a day, the next month you're writing 500 in an hour. As long as you keep moving, things begin to fall into place. With a collaborator acting as your accountability partner, you are *responsible* for someone else's success, too. That's enough to put heat under your feet and roll you in the right direction.

Yes, it may seem scary, but the reality is, you're not alone! Having a down-night and think you've got no more juice left in the tank? Here comes Phil with his Texas twang and a glassful of motivationade ready to let you know that he had a hard day, too, so maybe you can do it together and push that little bit harder. Maybe you jump on Skype. Maybe you call each other on the phone. Maybe you see the smoke signals on the horizon and wonder why nobody has called the fire brigade.

Having an accountability partner is as motivating for you as it is for them. I know for a fact that I would never have been able to put down the first 100,000 words of mine and Luke's novel, *Lazarus*, if I hadn't known that he was relying on me to finish.

Accountability is the equivalent of Michael Jordan's secret formula in *Space Jam*. There's no real magic, it's all in your head. But, still, somehow it works.

There's the rub. Can you put your own ego and fears aside and rely on someone else? More than that, can you become the type of writer someone else can rely on?

We're not even talking about mammoth projects, here, either. Don't want to commit to a full novel? Start on something small. Whatever you do, make sure you start and don't sit down until you finish. The worst thing you can do is disappear and leave your partner hanging. Unfortunately, it happens. If you do ever find yourself in that position, I refer you back to "2.2. Honesty is the only policy".

 "I had to step in on three different occasions and finish writing books myself because the collaborator disappeared. Don't ever ghost someone. Be honest if you can't do the work."

— CRAIG MARTELLE

2.5. CONTROL FREAKS

Despite the negative associations surrounding "control freaks", just because you *have* to be the admin of the document, and just because you *have* to have the final oversight of the finished draft, and just because you *have* to be the one to contact the cover designer, editor, manage the mailing list, liaise with the proofreaders, monitor the publication dashboards, and be the only one to click the publish button, doesn't mean you can't collaborate.

Some people are obsessed with control. That's fine. That can be useful. Some people want to only touch one part of the process, so there's room for you to take on the rest. Maybe your collaborator only wants to write the first draft and never see the damn thing again, that's also fine, too.

It's all fine. Everything's fine.
Breaths deeply into a paper bag

Control freaks can get a bad rep, but there is room in this arena for you, too. When it comes down to which levels of control you have in your collaboration, that's up for discussion at *the very beginning* of your collaboration.

Expectation-setting is *huge* and something that we discuss later in this book. As we've seen, collaborations rarely have to be an even split. If you love one part of the process, and you want to "Own it, baby," then own it. Find a collaborator who can deal with your impish obsessions of hyphenated words and use of conjunctions when slamming through the final draft and go nuts!

A word of caution to this tale.

While there is room for certain levels of operational control when it comes to processes and ensuring the work gets done, there are those who cannot quite let go enough to allow someone else into their process.

That's okay. That's fine. Collaboration may not be for you. If you love every step of the process, and you know that your livelihood is dependent on ensuring that *you* create quality work that represents *your* brand and pleases *your* readers, that's fine, too. This book isn't aimed at deluding the world into thinking that everyone should collaborate. The world needs the solo artists as well, and there are certain personality types out there that would rather drive two biros into their eyes than even contemplate the idea of letting someone into their inner sanctum of writerhood.

Everyone's different. Each collaboration is different. Have a good conversation with yourself and *be honest* about what you can and can't let go of before you approach someone to collaborate with.

And, who knows, somewhere down the line, you may find that you're ready and willing to let go of a lot more than you thought you could to begin with. Control in collaborations is all linked to trust. The more you trust someone, the easier it is to share.

2.6. TRUST

A quick word on trust.

I almost didn't include this as a section. It seems pretty obvious that trust *must* play a vital role in your collaboration. Without the "us", all you have is "trt", and what use is that?

Trust is that feeling in your gut when the waters are calm. When things are going well, there's not a ripple in that lake. Sure, someone may throw a stone once in a while and scare a few carp, but for the most part, all is serene.

You will know when a collaboration doesn't *feel* right. Those waters will turn wavier than a bowlful of jelly in an earthquake. Tides will swell and a deep-seated unease will churn in your stomach until you're churning enough to make butter.

Collaborations enforce one of the greatest trusting relationships there can be. You're relying on someone to do their part so that you both may succeed and rise as one. You're privy to work secrets and, often, you hold someone's precious and personal information in the palm of your hands.

If you can't trust the person you're collaborating with, you may as well build a house out of cotton candy. Wait for the rains to come and wash that shit away.

On the flip side, if *you* can't hold yourself wholly to account and be someone that someone else can trust, then back up before you do any damage. There's no way to fake your way through collaborations. The entire process is see-through. Sooner or later you'll get caught out and won't have anybody to cry to when the situation turns sour.

Trust is difficult to build and easy to lose.

Invaluable rewards are on the other side of trust, and when you meet the right collaborative partner, the whole notion of your collaboration transcends the work partner relationship and becomes something much more special.

2.7. MEET YOUR NEW SPOUSE

M an and woman, woman and woman, man and man, place your sexual preferences aside and stifle your schoolyard giggles, please.

Your collaborator can very quickly become something much more than a mere work colleague. You will be sharing workloads, you will be guiding yourselves towards a common goal, and you will open yourself up more than you ever have with someone you work with before. If you are working a full-time day job, then it's likely that you and your new collaborator will be talking at all hours of the day, squeezing in frantic idea sessions on the commute to work, calling each other late into the night to discuss launch strategies and financial management, giggling on the sofa during your movie on date night because you just *had* to send that meme to your writing partner.

I've been there. I've done it. I've spent hours on Skype, Zoom, and any other video conferencing software, putting in the hours to create something that I was proud of with someone I grew to care about. I would spend time with my partner, and then say an early goodnight to spend an hour or two deep into planning world-domination with my collaborators.

Of course, some of this is exaggeration, and the nature of your collaboration will be entirely individual. However, you need to be prepared to engage in something of a romantic relationship (minus the romance). In other words:

A relationship.

If I'm making it sound heavy, that's because it is. I'm going to make the sweeping assumption that you want to make this your full-time gig, or you at least want to put out quality content. If that is the case, then you need to take this seriously. Finding a collaborator who works for you is much like dating. Maintaining that connection and excitement for your project is no different to your Friday night dates with your spouse when you head to Wetherspoons followed by the Odeon (for my transatlantic readers, that's a meal followed by the movies). If you've read the other sections so far, then you already know you need to check your ego at the door, you need to be honest, you need to know your worth, you need to be accountable, and you need to build trust.

What difference is there, really, between building a lasting romantic relationship, and writing with a collaborative partner?

I know, I know. I meant besides the obvious, genius.

Each collaboration I've partaken in has thrown me in at the deep end with real people and real lives. You take calls and hear about their day, you support them through their troubles, and they support you, too. You schedule in regular meetings and make time for one another.

Because that's what it takes to make a collaboration successful.

Take your collaborator to the top of the mountain. Get down on one knee and make a sweeping declaration that you'll be there, by their side, forever—'til death do us part.

Or, at least until the project's done.

2.8. BUILDING A TRACK RECORD

"But I've never collaborated before."

"But I still haven't written my first novel."

"But I forgot to close the freezer for the fourth time this week, and now there's a puddle on my kitchen floor, PHIL!"

Okay, scrap that last one.

Building a track record is your secret sauce in this equation. If you can take those baby steps to prove that you're reliable and can finish a project, then you're on a roll. And, baby, once that ball stops rolling downhill, there's very little that can stop it.

When I'm approached by a potential collaborator, the first thing I do is look at what they've already done. Are they writing in my genre? Have they put out a decent amount of content in the last couple of years? Are there any red flags (see "5.3. Collaboration red flags") popping up that might mean that this won't work?

That's *my* process... usually. But that doesn't mean that there aren't exceptions to the rule.

The core component here is that you can prove that you can get things done. *Things*. Not necessarily books. I've collaborated with friends who work on film productions and want to get into writing prose. I've worked with collaborators who have only had a couple of short stories to their names. For me, if you can prove that you have some kind of quality to your writing, and that you can deliver when you say you will, then that's all there is to it.

Of course, the deeper you go down this rabbit hole, the greater the pool of experience and knowledge you may need. There's a lot of writers in the current climate looking at collaborators for anything from 3- to 21-book series. If you've only got a single short story to your name, you may have to look at reining in your ambition, and building up to that point. Collaborate on a few shorts. Work on a novella. Pump out a few novels. Start small.

 "Start with a short story or a novella, something very defined."

— J. Thorn

The beautiful thing about this game is that, no matter what level of author you consider yourself to be, there are thousands of writers in the same boat, within easy reach of those keyboard-calloused fingertips. Search in the right places and you'll find someone. Lurk in the right forums or stalk at the right conferences, and someone will pique your interest as a potential collaborator.

The point is, it's a numbers game. The primary ingredient that collaborators are looking for before throwing themselves into the ring with you is that you can deliver on your promises. You're there to help each other. You're there to hold each other up. It's supposed to be beneficial for both parties.

So, get to work building that foundation, prove to the hungry collaborators that you can deliver upon your promises (because you've done it a thousand times before) and collaborations will come flocking to you like mosquitos on a warm summer's eve.

2.9. "NO"

To clarify, the title of this section isn't the answer to the question posed at the beginning of this chapter:

"Is collaboration right for *you*?"

"*No.*"

Wouldn't that be a great way to close this book?

"No," is a powerful word. It's the shortest possible way to answer a question, and it leaves little ambiguity behind it.

"Mum, can I have a fiver?"

"No."

"I'd like one single to Jackson Drive, please."

"No."

"Excuse me, sir. Do you have a spare moment to talk about—"

"No."

"No" can hurt. It's blunt, it's direct, it's abrasive, yet it can also be your best friend.

Allow me to indulge once again in my "Collaboration is Dating" theory, as the analogy extends quite nicely to this section.

You may be buzzing with excitement at the possibility of

collaborating. You may have the perfect collaboration partner in mind, and you're foaming at the mouth to ask them. You may be waiting for a single "okay" from me to give you permission to pursue that one avenue that you've been toying with for the best part of six months.

You pick up the courage.

You drop the email. Or text. Or call. Whatever.

You read the dreaded word.

"No."

You throw your laptop at the wall, promise to never write another word again, and spend the next three decades working livestock on your cousin Maisy's farm, little realizing the blessing you've truly been given in that interaction.

As mentioned in the last section, it's all a numbers game. Much like with dating, you *will* get rejected.

You will.

Stop arguing with me. You will.

You will open yourself up to people and they will say no. That one collaborator that you think *can't* say no, does. And then what happens?

You keep trying.

To be rejected by a potential collaborator is a goddamn blessing!

To collaborate with someone who doesn't truly want to collaborate with you is hard work, believe me. There's nothing worse than feeling like you're the only one invested in your project while the other person is dragging their heels, missing deadlines, and constantly telling you it's their *next* priority.

Similar with dating. The hot stranger who said "no" doesn't want you. That's great to know! Why would you want to be with someone who doesn't want you back? What kind of self-effacing monster wants to spend their dying years in the arms of a potential lover who accepts seven tequila shots for free and *still* says no?

"No" is a powerful word in collaboration. It can save you heartache, and it can give you direction. You don't want that person who says "no". You want the person who says "yes", and sometimes that takes time. You cannot rush a collaboration. You cannot force a partner to engage in something they are not comfortable with.

Maybe they're not at the same point in their author journey as you thought they were. Maybe they're already knee deep in another project and don't have time. Maybe their goals don't align and it's something they just don't want to do.

When asked if he's ever said no to a potential collaboration before, Luke Kondor said, "If I have, it would have been if I wasn't excited about the project or if I didn't have the time to invest."

It all comes down to being honest. Not everyone is in the same position as you.

Be glad you heard the "no".

Be prepared for the "no".

But don't let it stop you reaching out and asking. Because, there's always a chance that they may say "yes".

That's how all of my collaborations have started. I've reached out and extended the offer. I've been prepared for the no, but also known that the only way you're 100% guaranteed a "no" is when you don't ask.

Remember: sometimes, people do say "yes".

2.10. THE COLLABORATION EQUATION

Collaboration isn't an exact science. As we've established, each collaboration is individual. There is no blanket template to collaborate with someone.

That said, there is a very basic equation that identifies and exploits the key parameters that can define whether or not a collaboration is on the cards.

First, we need to look at a few key terms. These are "needs", "wants" and "opportunities".

Needs

Without a need, what's the point? The need could be a number of things and will be unique and individual to each person's situation.

A need is a primal urge, it's a drive, it's a compulsion. A need is something you *have* to have, and it can accelerate any collaboration if utilized correctly.

A few examples of needs in making a career from writing could be:

- Financial well-being (needing enough moolah to pay the rent; not being able to afford the start-up costs for covers, editors, etc.)
- An overload of demand (needing others to help feed the hungry mouths of their audience; being overly ambitious and stuck, etc.)
- Tight, contracted deadlines (someone has overstretched themselves and promised a fast turnaround, now they need you to write for them)

Wants

Wants are different to needs (not that some people know the difference). A want is a nicety. It's something you *could* do without, but you'd prefer if you could obtain. In life, a want could be upgrading your television to a new 50" unit. Whereas, the need would be being able to afford electricity so you can keep your family warm and toasty in front of your current 47" screen.

A lot of collaborations spring from wants. Most people want to write more, most people want to have another writer support them, a lot of people just *want* to try it.

Wants are a bit woollier than needs. If there's a need for someone to collaborate, you're more likely to secure that deal. If somebody wants to, then you're in with a good chance of making it happen, but it's not entirely essential, and sometimes these can fizzle out.

A few examples of wants could be:

- Learning opportunities (having zero clue how to write in a genre, but willing to learn; wanting to gain specific skills to reach the next level of your author career, etc.)
- Peer support (desiring the company of others so you

don't feel so lonely along the journey; wanting confirmation and reassurance of the quality of what you're writing)

- Riding the waves of someone's name (you want to boost your own career by writing with a big named author who's asking).

Opportunities

This is where we bring the motivations together. It doesn't matter whether your collaboration is a want or a need, there needs to be an opportunity for it to happen.

The collaborative opportunity can vary greatly (as we'll go into in the next chapter), but without opportunity, there's no collaboration. No matter how much you *want* something to happen, the other parameters need to exist. *You* may want to feed your kids with the money you make from a collaboration, but it doesn't matter how much you want or need it, without the opportunity, it'll never happen.

That doesn't mean you can't make your own opportunities, of course. But, likewise, if no one wants or needs you, you're riding solo, boss.

Need (or) Want + Opportunity = Collaboration

Simple, really.

2.11. EXPERT PANEL

WHAT DO YOU LOOK FOR IN A COLLABORATOR?

When asking my expert panel about what qualities they look for in a collaborative partner, I received a whole slew of fantastic answers to help guide you.

Here are just a few of the responses I gathered from some of the independent author community's most successful collaborators.

> *Easy to get along with. Not precious about their words. Able to deliver constructive feedback. Able to take feedback. Punctual.*
>
> — RAMY VANCE

> *Quality of story first and trust. They have to be able to deliver when they say they're going to deliver, and they have to write good words. Trust means you say what you're going to do and then you do it.*
>
> — CRAIG MARTELLE

Personality, professionalism, punctuality, performance.

— MICHAEL ANDERLE

Same philosophical outlook. Lack of ego. Commitment to best product.

— NICK COLE

Fun, drama free, consistent, reliable.

— JONATHAN YANEZ

A healthy balance of give and take.

— LUKE KONDOR

2.12. SUMMARY

- **Is collaboration for you?** Figure out your reasons for collaborating ahead of time and be realistic with what you're hoping to achieve. Collaboration *isn't* for everyone, but it can be an avenue for a *lot* of writers.
- **Ego.** There's no place in collaborations for egos, you are partners on even keels. You need to be able to put ego aside and put the story first in order to make this work. Work together, work fairly, and work with due respect for each other.
- **Honesty.** Honesty is the *only* way to make a collaboration work. You need to be honest with yourself about what you want; you need to be honest with your potential partner about what you hope to gain and what experience you have; you need to be honest with yourself every step of the way if you're going to make this work.
- **Knowing your worth.** Collaborations should never make you feel lesser or insignificant. Know your

value and enter through the collaboration doorway with pride and a confidence that you can contribute fairly to the project.

- **Accountability.** Deliver on your promises, someone else depends on it. Lean on your collaborator when you need to, and let them lean on you, and don't overstretch on your promises.
- **Control freaks.** Yes, even control freaks can collaborate. If you *are* a control freak, then be honest and upfront about it and find a way to navigate this plain. Set your boundaries of what you are and aren't willing to do and ensure that those expectations are established from the get-go.
- **Trust.** Trust your gut, ensure that you can trust your partner, and ensure that you are also trustworthy. Trust is the sticky residue that holds the arc together; without it you're left washed away on flotsam.
- **Your new spouse.** Collaborative partnerships can be compared to romantic relationships, sans romance. You will spend a *lot* of time in contact with your collaborative partner if you're going to make this work. Make sure you choose the right person to invest your time in.
- **Building a track record.** Start small and build a track record—a writer's CV, if you will. Most collaborators look at an author's backlist to confirm that their potential partner is writing. It doesn't have to be big, but don't leave a trail of failures and broken promises behind you.
- **"No".** Get used to this word. It can hurt, but you may hear a lot of them. That's okay, keep striking the rock until it bleeds gold. Sometimes that takes time.

- **The collaboration equation.** Need (or) Want +
  Opportunity = Collaboration. Without the
  opportunity, or without the need/want, you have no
  collaboration.

COLLABORATION CASE STUDY: J. THORN AND ZACH BOHANNON

J. Thorn and Zach Bohannon are the indie powerhouses behind the post-apocalyptic and dystopian publishing company, Molten Universe Media.

Together, J. and Zach have co-authored over a dozen books. They've coordinated numerous fiction anthologies with fellow writers who have partaken in their unique in-person author events, including their renowned "Authors on a Train" experience. They are the co-hosts of *The Career Author* podcast, the faces of The Career Author summit, and the brains behind the non-fiction *Three-Story Method*.

Not only do I have the privilege of calling this duo my friends, they were also kind enough to donate some time to answer some burning questions I had about how they view collaboration.

One thing I found particularly useful from this conversation is that it shows the evolution of the collaboration process over time. Collaboration can be a path to self-discovery, and sometimes what you want out of a collaboration changes over time. That is highlighted here.

. . .

DAN: How would you describe the nature of your collaboration?

J.: Our core collaborative structure is co-writing. The way we define it, and the way we've done it for 12+ books is an equal share of both investment and profit.

And that changes, you know? We've gone through different phases. What's important to recognize for us is that we don't necessarily do the exact same process twice and we're not being counters. We're not, "Well, I wrote 100 words and so now you must write 100 words." We play off on our strengths.

Traditionally, my strength is revision and drafts, and Zach's is first-drafting. But even within that, we send things back and forth to each other. Sometimes we've worked on projects completely independent of each other and then had some input later on.

So, we don't necessarily have a format that we use the same way every time.

DAN: How did you first begin collaborating?

ZACH: It was around the time I started wanting to get into writing that I found J's podcast and became a fan of his books.

We ended up emailing each other and soon figured out that we had a lot of stuff in common, beyond even just the books we both liked. We liked a lot of the same music and we just had similar lifestyles as well. We ended up doing the "Horror Writers Podcast" together, and it had come up about writing a book together, but we never really rushed into it. We had one or two projects that we thought about doing that kind of fell by the wayside, and then we eventually came across an idea that we wanted to do.

By that time, we had become friends and been talking for a year, or so. So, it wasn't something we necessarily rushed into and I think that's part of the reason that our partnership has gone on and transcended, because we didn't just talk for five minutes in a Facebook group and then be like, "Oh, we write the same thing. We should write a book together." Which is fine for some people. Some people make that work and they might just want to do one or two books together. But if you're looking at doing a longer-term thing like we wanted to do then this kind of worked out better for us that way.

J.: I didn't think too much about it because Zach and I both have a background of being musicians in bands, and that's just how bands operate. They're just collaborative by nature. So, it wasn't something I felt like I had to try. It was like, "Well, no, this is how art is made. You make art with other people."

DAN: How has your collaboration affected your individual work? Has it had any impact outside of collaboration?

ZACH: I've discovered that I'm very much a one-project-at-a-time person. I end up having to put a lot of my own stuff on the backburner.

It's really hard for me to be juggling multiple projects at a time. If I was in a groove where I was revising one book and then first-drafting another, that would be one thing. But if I'm trying to first-draft two projects at the same time, or revise two projects, that's hard for me. I really like to get one book done, put it away, go to the next one. So, it's affected my personal stuff a lot over the last few years and we're actually coming to a place where we're going to co-write fiction a little bit less partly because of that, and partly because J's looking at some different things in a different direction and I'm wanting to go and take care of some of my own stuff for a while.

I've learned enough that, as much as I want to tell myself I can still have my own books, I can't [during a collaboration] so we're shifting some things around in our business right now where we're going to be focusing more on our own stuff but for me it's really a one project at a time thing and I know J's a little bit he can give you a different answer.

J.: Yeah, I'm the complete opposite. I find it incredibly difficult to work on one thing at a time. I lose interest. I get fatigued. So, I like to have change and variety. I don't like to do 15 different things in one day, but over the course of a week, I like to be in two to three different projects. I might spend a whole day on one, but I can't spend the whole week on one. So, for me it was a much easier fit and had much less of an impact on my individual stuff because it was just one of several things that I had operating all at the same time.

DAN: What qualities do you look for in a collaborator?

J.: Disposition is something that you should pay attention to. You want a co-writer or collaborator to have the same general disposition as you.

For example, if you are a really anxious person, you probably don't want to pair up with someone who's really laid back and doesn't care a lot about stuff, because there's going to be an inherent conflict there. If you're both ambitious, or if it's a passion project for both of you, then that would be a good alignment.

The flip side to that is that you want to be looking for someone who has a different skill set than you do. Whether that's drafting versus revising, whether that is craft versus marketing, there are certain spectrums and different ends of the spectrum. If you're strong in one area, you want to look for someone who's as complementarily strong in the other area—but also while your dispositions match. So, it's a bit of an odd pairing, because you want to find someone who's like you, but not.

DAN: Have you ever been in a situation when you've had to say "no" to a potential collaborator?

J.: One of my red flags is someone who offers something that requires me to do most of the work. You wouldn't think you'd get pitches like that, but you absolutely do. I think too, for me, it's kind of odd because I don't have a career-breaking platform. But there are some people who think, "Oh, if I just write with that guy, then the floodgates will open, and the royalties will rain down." I can sniff out those emails.

Overuse of flattery is another thing. It's obvious when people don't know me very well, and they try and pretend that they do. So, if they found one book and they skim the Amazon description and then write, "Oh, I really love that book that had that character in it, by the way. So, here's what I'm thinking." If you had done the research you would know I'm not a James Patterson, you're not going to put my name on the book and all of a sudden, it's going to fly off the shelves. But I can tell when people don't know me very well, because they just glance over something that they could find on the Amazon author page, and then they just get right into their pitch. That's a big indicator for me.

DAN: What's one thing that you hear about collaboration that just isn't true?

ZACH: One misconception is that writing together is going to mean you're going to get stuff done faster. And that's not the case, necessarily. It doesn't necessarily mean you're going to get books out a lot faster.

DAN: Have you guys tackled any situations where the collaboration was in jeopardy or it didn't match your expectations?

ZACH: For me, it's just about communication. I'm not the type person who really likes to hold things in. So, if I'm feeling a way, I'll definitely say, "Hey, we need to talk."

There's no wall we've had that just a conversation and actually talking through it did not work out—preferably in person, if you're able to. Talking in person is way better. That's the biggest thing. You just have to be really open and communicate and not really hold anything back and you have to recognize, like I've had to recognize, for instance, that I can't work on multiple projects, as much as I want to try to become that person. It's not going to happen. So, once I recognized that, I was like, "Okay, now we need to sit down and have a talk. We need to figure some stuff out."

J.: It goes back to this idea of having a similar disposition. Neither Zach nor I are precious about our words or our stories or ideas. Some people are, and that's fine. But, if we bring an idea to the table and the other person doesn't like it, we're like, "Okay. Well, then, fine. Let's do something else." For us, it's about the story. It's putting the story first. And, maybe this gets back to the idea of leaving the ego at the door, we just say, "Okay, well, if that's not the best idea, then then we'll come up with a better one".

DAN: How important are contracts and agreements to a collaborative project?

J.: I wouldn't enter into a collaboration without one. It doesn't have to be complicated and you don't necessarily need to involve a team of lawyers, but I would not enter into any kind of collaboration without a written agreement.

DAN: Are there any software packages or systems that are fundamental to your collaboration?

ZACH: We pretty much use Google Drive and Slack and Zoom

for everything. That's pretty much it. We do our drafts in Google Drive. Our files are in Google Drive. We don't use email to chat with each other. All of that's done through Slack, and then if we need video conferencing, we use Zoom.

J.: I think authors tend to overcomplicate things. You don't need a tonne of fancy tools. I'm a big fan of Scrivener, and I use that when I first draft my own projects, but as it currently is, that software is not easy for collaborators because you have issues of overwriting things and backing up and managing versions of documents. So, exactly like Zack said, we try and keep it as simple and streamlined as possible.

DAN: What one piece of advice would you give to someone looking to get involved in their first collaborative project?

J.: Start small. Start with a short story or a novella, something very defined. I've talked a number of times about how most of my collaborations have failed, but you don't see the failures because most of them haven't produced anything. So, be very, very realistic, and keep it very small-scale when you first meet someone because it's easy to run away with ideas.

ZACH: You can come up with a bunch of really cool ideas together. But if you get into the process and things start falling apart, none of that's going to matter. Starting with a short story or doing a few short stories or a novella or something like J. said, is a really good way to test the waters and see how you're going to work with somebody else.

I would also add that you should try to work with someone who has similar experience to you. If you've published a few books, and you are working with a first-time author who's never even worked with an editor before, that could have some challenges with it.

PART III

TYPES OF COLLABORATION

3. TYPES OF COLLABORATION

Here's where we ready our mouth bones and chomp into the juicy chunks of collaboration.

Up until this point, I've mostly referred to collaborations as their general whole. We've explored what it takes for a person to succeed in collaborations, and the mental and psychological considerations which come as part and parcel to every collaborative effort.

And I mean "every".

There is a metric crap tonne of individual collaboration types out there. I'll repeat my mantra here: "every collaboration is an individual process". There is no "one way" to collaborate. There is no "perfect" way to partner with someone and get it done. As much as we'd *love* a perfect formula, there is none. All that exists are needs and wants.

And opportunities. Let's not forget the multitude of opportunities.

That said, there are a few umbrella collaborations which are commonly seen in the world of authorship. These I'll go into over the next few sections in more detail so that you can take a glance and see which of these suits your fancy.

We'll explore the "how" of collaboration in much more detail later in the book, but first, let's lay out the overview of each type of collaboration, so that all the terminology and concepts are covered.

3.1. CO-WRITING

I'm more than likely to fall off my chair in a dizzying spell of wonder if you tell me that you've never heard of the concept of co-writing.

A vast majority of writers confuse co-writing to encompass the word "collaboration".

All forms of co-writing *are* collaboration, but not all collaborations are co-writing.

Co-writing means that there are significant inputs into a product by both parties. You and your collaborator are creating the content. You're both sprinkling your special sauce onto the page in one way or another, and you're both inputting *something* into the finished book. That could take the shape of:

- Writing a one-off novel between two of you
- Creating a series from scratch
- Writing in someone else's world but both contributing significant efforts to the story

- Allowing someone to write in your world and being hands-on in the story that's told

In most of these cases, the final product is going to end up with a pair of names on the front cover. If you've both put in equal effort to write the book, then you'll want to get the credit you deserve, right?

However, there are some exceptions. By writing in someone else's world, the world's creator may be graceful enough to allow you to have your own name on the cover, sans creator. You've co-written, because they've set the scene and the ideas behind the world, but the story itself is yours.

Unlike some of the other forms of collaboration, this one can sometimes seem a little more difficult to grasp. So, let me take some examples of co-writing and flesh them out in more detail.

3.1.1. ONE-OFFS

One-offs are the perfect way to dip your toes into the metaphorical collaboration pond (watch out for leeches).

With one-off collaborations, you are setting a very simple expectation:

- You are going to commit to something small
- There is less pressure
- If this doesn't work, you've got an out
- If this *does* work, you've got an option to renegotiate and continue

What is there to lose?

As J. and Zach mentioned in the previous case study, you don't even have to start with a full book or novel. If you're already quivering with fear and not sure that you've got what it takes to lay 60,000 word bricks to build a novel mansion, then write a short story. Produce a 2,000-word short, or a piece of flash fiction that you and your collaborator can send into magazines or online blogs or anthologies.

A one-off collaboration is the ultimate starting point, and that extends beyond virgin collaborators. Even a writer like myself, who has dealt mostly with collaborations in my own work for half a decade, offers small, one-off projects when looking at getting collaborations with *new* partners. If someone doesn't already have a track record of writing with other people but has produced their own work solidly for a length of time, then hell yeah, I'm going to give it a go. What's the worst that can happen?

One-offs are the equivalent of speed-dates (in my very limited experience of the rapid dating pool). You follow the rules, you learn enough about a partner to decide whether to continue with the relationship or not, and you move on. It's as simple as that.

The great thing is that you don't even have to just commit to a single one-off. If you're feeling particularly randy and would like to dabble at polygamous collaborations (you lucky devil, you), then you can find a way to juggle multiple collaborations at once and speed up your overall chances of finding a collaboration that works.

A word of warning: take it slow to start with. Polygamy is better left to the experienced, unless you want to find yourself with an overwhelming to-do pile as ten different collaboration projects find their way back to you all at once. Not speaking from experience, or anything.

The one-off is where I'd advise beginners to start, and also what I'd suggest that the experienced try with new partners. You can launch into planning a series together, but if you run into obstacles on the first book, all of that planning, hope and expectation just goes straight out the window.

Pros

- Great for first-time collaborators to test the waters
- Perfect for testing a collaboration with a new partner
- If a project doesn't sell, you can move on quickly
- Less allocated time resource to planning and production
- A good way to test multiple collaborators at once

Cons

- Slower to build momentum if you're looking to plan a series
- Difficult to manage if you take on too many at once
- Can give you false hope if someone is on their best behaviour on a short project, then reveals their true nature on a larger project

3.1.2. SHARING YOUR OWN UNIVERSE

Creation of an entire story universe is a big ask, but it's also one of the most popular forms of collaboration right now.

Consider this: you have a series that's hit a considerable number of downloads. You're seeing returns on your creation, and you know that people are responding positively to it. You have a thousand ideas for stories you could create in your universe, but you are just one person. You need to feed coal to the locomotive to keep it going, but you just can't do it alone.

That's where sharing your universe comes in.

If you're one of the lucky ones to have found this kind of success, you're likely going to have a story bible detailing the rules and restrictions of your universe. Elves are blue, dwarves' thumbs are too fat to text, that kind of thing. Armed with that information, you can open the doors to other writers to join in and help create properties that not only feed your hungry readers, but also grow the world and benefit your collaborator, too.

There are dozens of examples of this kind of story expansion right now. Michael Anderle's "The Kurtherian Gambit", Garrett Robinson's "Underrealm" universe, Ramy Vance's "GoneGod World" are just a few.

If you've got a story that's chomping at the bit, waiting to accelerate and provide your readers with some quality content, all you need to do is open the flood gates.

But how do I ensure that my collaborators know my universe as well as I do and deliver a quality experience to my readers?

This is a big question, but it has a few easy solutions, depending on how you want to move forward.

Monitoring someone's story as they write in your universe can take a lot of time and effort to ensure that they're keeping on the right track. When someone's writing in your world, there's always the worry that they're going off on tangents and creating rules that wouldn't necessarily be true to what you'd envisioned for your world.

There are two ways to tackle this:

1. You check in at regular intervals, looking at an agreed amount of words in advance (for example, look over every 5,000 words before you continue), and help to answer any questions your co-writer may have so they may continue in a manner that you're happy with.
2. You set clear guidelines at the very beginning, be as explicit as possible, trust the process, and review the story at the end.

Either way, you're going to have to have some kind of input into this project. Whether that's a final read, or a chapter-by-chapter review, the onus is on you to make sure that your co-writer is hitting the tone and pace of the stories *you* want to tell.

The truth is that in opening up your universe, you *won't* have control over everything. Do you think people would want to write in your universe if you're giving them step-by-step instructions and putting in hard red lines at every corner?

Be true to your property (it is *your* universe, after all), but allow some flexibility. Sometimes you may discover that your collaborators have an idea that comes from so far out of left field that it knocks the air out of your wheezing, asthmatic stomach. Yet, it could still be one of the greatest ideas to ever grace your universe, and your fans could love it.

Be open, be honest, but, most of all, be true.

Pro tip: Use your fans

This one hit me like a friggin' bolt of lightning when I first saw others doing this.

Fans of your work can make the best collaborators.

Think about it, you have a pool of hundreds of readers. These readers reach out to you, shout adorations of your work from the rooftops, debate which kind of breakfast cereal your protagonist would eat if they lived in the modern world, know the color of mascara your heroine prefers when she's not on a budget.

They already have the story bible in their head. They've consumed all of your works and know the tone and the tempo of every line and paragraph. Maybe there's a writer among that group. Maybe that writer is looking for their big break. Maybe you reach out and offer them a trial.

Reaching out to fans could be a shortcut to getting quality work in your universe. Not only that, but they'll be eternally grateful for the opportunity to contribute to something they love, and that will make them one of, what Kevin Kelly calls, your "1,000 true fans".

It might seem daunting at first. But, be honest, isn't it just a little tempting?

Pros

- Increase the volume of books within your universe
- Meet the demand of hungry readers faster
- Open yourself up to new ideas and directions for your universe
- Readers like the familiar, the more books there are within an established universe, the more likely they are to invest
- A great chance to upgrade fans to super fans if you invite them to write with you

Cons

- A potential to lose a grip on your original concept and disappoint readers
- One bad product can negatively affect all your work
- Collaborations can require a lot of maintenance and direct contact, especially in the beginning

3.1.3. PLAYING IN SOMEONE ELSE'S SANDPIT

Let's be honest. There are already so many fantastic books out there, raking in the downloads and capturing the reader's attention, why bother trying to carve your own particular niche in the bedrock of fiction when you can jump in on someone else's success?

Of course, this is a sweeping generalization of the book industry, but you've got to admit, there is some merit there.

As we've covered, while playing in someone else's sandpit (universe) may not have you topping the charts and—for those still employed in a full-time position—throwing your resignation in your boss's face, it will still be a sure-fire way to raise your platform and get your name out into the pool of writers that readers should care about. By jumping into someone else's universe, you are erasing the need to learn a lot of the most painful mistakes you can make when you are an established author:

- You don't have to worry as much about building your own readership (there should already be an existing one there)

- The world is already built, all you've got to do is find the story to add your unique flair
- You're writing with an already established writer and that will add further merit to your name

By writing in someone else's universe, all you've got to worry about is crafting a solid story. Craft a great story and tick all the genre and story boxes, fulfil reader expectations, don't be a dick, and you'll be just fine.

However, as my seedy uncle, John, used to tell me every Friday after his weekly visit to a very particular neon bar, there's always a "but".

While writing within someone else's universe is a great way to get your name established among other writers (and some readers, too), the readership of that particular universe are often hungry for more stories within that particular universe.

If, after some stretch of time, you close your book or series and feel like hopping into your own work, you'll find that you can't *rely* on every one of those readers diving straight into your particular backlist. Don't get me wrong, people *will* convert, but you won't be able to inherit every single reader from that collaboration.

I know. It sucks, right?

Believe me, I've been there. You jump out of the series and think the world is going to bow at your feet and your fleet of readers are going to dive into the ocean and find their footing upon your own private cruise-liner, but instead you've only got enough to fill a dinghy.

And then, what? All that work you've done with someone else, writing in their universe, and spending hours playing with their characters amounts to naught.

I'm being overdramatic, here. While the above can certainly be true, it wouldn't have been worth mentioning without its benefits. By writing in someone else's established universe, you *have* shortcut a lot of the groundwork of writership, maybe you've learned a load of publishing lessons you'd never have learned alone, but it can often be tricky to try and build that reader base if you're not at least doing something of your own work.

Pros

- You don't have to go through the hard work of finding readers, they're already there!
- You spend less time world building, and more time story-crafting
- You're associating your name with an already established writer and building reader trust
- You're fast-tracking your portfolio of work
- You can watch and learn from a writer who is already making a success of it so you can apply this to your own work

Cons

- While you're writing in someone else's world, you're not building your own IPs
- It can be unlikely that your collaborator's readers will follow you into your own work
- Your creativity relies on the permissions of the universe's originator

3.2. PUBLISHING PARTNERSHIPS

W e've established the particulars of co-writing and the operational ways that that can work for people, but now let's dive into the deep stuff.

Sharing a publishing house.

Becoming business partners.

Legally binding yourself to another writer in more than just books.

It all sounds pretty scary, huh? The idea that you can own a business that publishes books and be 50% responsible for everything that comes in and out of that business.

Running a publishing company is not for everyone. If you're not in the mindset of making time to understand financial accounts, study the art of marketing, manage clients and properties, pay taxes, and look after intellectual properties, then just skip this section.

Then put the book down.

Seriously. Put it down, now. Because everything listed above is exactly what we're already doing anyway, particularly if you're an independent author (maybe not so if you're hoping for a traditional publishing deal, in which case *you* may skip this section). You're already managing a small business. The government is already watching your income. You're already in charge of promoting your book and handling your finances.

The only difference here, is that you are binding yourself to someone else. You are placing your bets on another writer and working together to inflate your chances of survival. If you suddenly hit mass success, great, you *both* benefit. If your collaborative partner hits mass success, amazing, you *both* benefit.

Collaborating on a publishing house is an expert-level partnership. Usually you'll find that those who join in on this kind of venture have been in the game a while and understand how the dice rolls. Business partnerships can seem burdensome, but if you're in it with someone you trust, and you know you both want to see each other succeed, then this could be one for you.

I'm one of four directors of a story studio called Hawk & Cleaver. When Luke Kondor, Ben Errington, Matt Butcher, and I founded the company in 2015, we knew we wanted to make stories and we knew we had similar interests in publishing. We wanted to break out of isolation as writers and rise together.

"A rising tide raises all ships"—have I said that already?

This little phrase became our manifesto. We created the publishing house to publish our books, our podcasts, and our comics together, and over the years we've built up a very modest audience, with certain properties accelerating a lot faster than others.

Publishing houses are great if you and your collaborators have a shared vision. They work when you're in direct communication and you're honest with what you're trying to achieve. You can share your victories, you can lament your failures, you're bound to other humans, and they're there to support you in much the same way as you are going to be there to support them. Publishing partnerships fall apart when people lie, when people become unreliable, and when people don't fulfil their promises.

When I spoke earlier about adopting a new spouse, this is the kind of collaboration where that rings truer than anything else. You are married to your collaborator, and you're promising that you'll be there to help them make a go of this venture.

And, just like some marriages, some collaborations drift apart. After a few years with each other, learning and growing as individuals, you might find that your goals and visions no longer align with the others'. Like any good relationship, check in regularly with each other, be honest, adhere to the sections in Chapter 2, and, if the time should come, part gracefully and with your head held high.

With this kind of partnership, you don't have to write in each other's worlds, you don't have to write the same books, you don't have to share anything but a vision and a bank account. For flexibility in your own writing, with reassurance that you're increasing your chances of overall success, this could be the avenue for you.

Publishing partnerships can be one of the greatest collaborations you ever enter into, just don't enter this one lightly.

Pros

- You have support along the author journey
- If one person succeeds, you both succeed
- You are creating something bigger than your work as individuals

- Your creativity in individual projects stays intact (as long as it meets the shared vision for your company)
- You already have the foundations laid if you'd like to expand and take on other authors

Cons

- If you're a first-time author, this option may seem intimidating
- You're legally responsible for another person's contribution to the business
- You *must* have a great grasp of business, finance, and marketing. None of that, "I think I do"

3.3. GHOSTWRITING

Yes, I may be a horror writer, but that's definitely not the kind of ghosts I'm talking about.

A lot of people might seem surprised to see ghostwriting in a book about collaboration. "Surely," you'll be shouting at your Kindle, "ghostwriting is a contractual exchange of services. There's nothing collaborative in the slightest!"

To that I say, "Calm down, enraged reader. You've scared the pigeons and Mrs Henderson is staring at you through the window."

Ghostwriting, by its very nature, is *collaborative*. Sure, you may not be in a position at the end where the ghostwriter claims credit for the project, but the whole notion of it involves two parties, inputting into a final product that is sold to the market.

Remember when we explored the collaboration equation earlier?

Need (or) Want + Opportunity = Collaboration

Ghostwriting is no different. Need or want (someone wanting to write for a living who doesn't care about taking the credit) + opportunity (someone looking for someone to write words under their name or brand) = collaboration (ghostwriting).

Ghostwriting is like Marmite for a lot of people. Among the writers within my circles, ghostwriting is seen as the final resort of the desperate, antiquated writer. If you're offering your talents out for ghostwriting, then you're doing yourself a disservice and giving up before you've even tried, they say. If you're looking to hire a ghostwriter, you're abusing the system and cheating your way to the top, say the others.

No matter your feelings about ghostwriting, the fact is that it can be an amazing opportunity for all involved. As with collaborations, all ghostwriting opportunities are individual. I've known of some ghostwriters who have a vast amount of input into the overall story idea of their client. I've known clients who could not be happier to provide an opportunity for fantastic writers to flourish, while protecting their identity.

 I stumbled across a webinar for how to make six figures through ghostwriting fiction. Once I learned that this was a viable option for me (plus how possible it was and how much money I could potentially make doing nothing but living my dream of writing fiction full-time), I dove into the opportunity head-first.

— KATHRIN HUTSON

The ghostwriter

Put your own ego aside when judging ghostwriters. You don't know their situations. Some ghostwriters love the *art of writing* but would rather stay anonymous. Some ghostwriters love the opportunity to write for chart-topping authors wanting to grow their products but protect their brand.

Ghostwriting can seem intimidating, yet it can be no different to any other kind of salaried position. A lot of ghost-writers offset their personal author careers with ghostwriting, using it as an opportunity to train from those who are ahead on the journey so they can become the best authors they can be. "I have learned *so* much about different styles of writing, different tropes in a variety of genres, and a whole new world of 'what readers want' through collaborating on and ghostwriting so many books for clients," says best-selling author, Kathrin Hutson.

There's a lot of skill that is needed to ghostwrite successfully. Akin to copywriting, ghostwriting requires that you master the art of "voice". When writing for a client, you are not writing your own brand of story (generally speaking), but you are often required to morph your tone and match that of your client's other works.

This can be a challenge for some, but it's also a great oppor-tunity to find the things that can work for their audience and bring them into your own work. Imagine being a thriller writer and having the chance to ghostwrite for James Patterson. Would you say no?

The downside, of course, is that while you are pumping your words into someone else's coal fire, your own kiln could be dwindling. Ghostwriting doesn't often serve much return in the way of credit, so it can seem like a pointless endeavour if you're looking to blow your own pipes. However, if you can manage ghostwriting alongside your own writing career, it could be a good way to build a stable platform for your business over time.

Think carefully before pursuing this as an avenue. Out of all the forms of collaboration, I think this one has the starkest contrasts between the benefits and the negatives.

The client

Let's examine the other side of the coin.

If you're interested in hiring a ghostwriter to help you, that usually means one of two things:

1. You're already super successful (lucky you) and you want to generate more fiction to feed your hungry readers, but aren't quite ready to enter the symbiotic relationship of a conventional co-writing agreement, whilst simultaneously wanting to protect your brand and all that you've worked on up to this point.
2. You can't write to save your life, but you have some incredible ideas, and a lot of cash.

That's a fairly black and white assessment, but it serves to illustrate the two main reasons, both of which require a stark injection of moolah, and a coveting and protecting of your personal brand.

Personal brand

Your personal brand is one of the fundamental aspects of your writing business that you need to protect. For some, co-writing with other authors runs the risk of watering their brand and confusing their readers. By hiring a ghostwriter, an author can maintain full control over their end product, and also increase their overall outputs of work. Don't get me wrong, by working with ghostwriters, you encounter a lot of the negatives associated with co-writing with someone else (extra time needed to ensure a quality product is produced), but you also have ultimate control over which way the story is going to go.

After all, it's going to be released with *your* name on.

Money, money, money

Ideally, if you're looking to hire a good ghostwriter, you're going to need a good wad of cash. Just in case I didn't emphasize the two key parts of that sentence enough, let me repeat: if you're looking to hire a *good* ghostwriter, you're going to need a *good wad* of cash.

Good ghostwriters can be worth every penny, but they can be expensive, too. When approaching a ghostwriter, don't waste yours and their time by offering a pittance for their services. In this transaction, they're offering you a lot more than you're offering them.

Sure, the money could go a *long* way to helping some ghostwriters, but without them, could you keep up with demand? Could you feed your readers? Could you put your "must write" ideas into logical, cohesive sentences in a way that will keep the reader's eyes glued to your pages, both digital and print?

Having ghostwritten myself, I've seen clients not setting expectations on what they're after, underpaying, stretching out work, and treating ghosts like crap.

Don't be that guy.

Money talks, and so do ghostwriters. Make sure you're paying fairly. Look after your ghosts. Sooner or later, they all come back to haunt you.

Dan steps off his soap box

Ultimately, ghostwriting is beneficial for a lot of reasons, though it also can be risky, too. My number one piece of advice for both ghosts and their clients—have an iron clad NDA (non-disclosure agreement) and play nicely.

That is all.

Pros (Ghostwriter)

- Guaranteed income with your writing
- Great opportunity to learn writing styles and voice from successful authors
- You can call yourself a writer without all the glam and recognition

Pros (Client)

- More products on the market with *your* name on
- Faster production
- You can write less

Cons (Ghostwriter)

- Distracts from your own work
- No recognition or public credit
- Mismanaged agreements with client can waste a lot of time

Cons (Client)

- Can be quite labour intensive
- Can be expensive
- Mismanaged agreements with ghostwriter can waste a lot of your time

3.4 ACCOUNTABILITY PARTNERS

Collaboration isn't all about the end product. Sometimes it's more than two people working on one thing together and raising the finished article high into the clouds shouting, "Hallelujah!"

Sometimes, collaboration can be as simple as helping hold someone to account, as they do the same for you.

I struggle to count on my fingers and toes how many writers I know who employ this kind of collaboration in their own work. They'd grown tired of missing their own deadlines, never hitting their goals, and staring at a blank page, and finally ended up finding someone else in the same position that they were in, so they could make a change.

Accountability partners are great, and they're not limited to any number. Accountability partners can be found in your writer's group, through social media, and specifically in online groups.

Accountability partners can be the kick up the backside that you need. They can give you a nudge on the days you're feeling like you've got nothing to give, and they can give you a boost towards your goals. Being surrounded by other writers going through the same thing you are is a tremendous bonus, and you may just find that you're capable of much more than you think you are.

However, I must make something very clear...

Even with accountability partners, *your* success is defined by *your* actions.

I've done it myself, on many occasions. Promised myself and a partner that I'd complete the chapter or write a set amount of words and not delivered. When the partner held me to account, did I tell the truth?

The hell I did! Well, at least not at first. The white lies caught up with me in the end.

Accountability partners are only worth the effort that you put into them. It's great holding someone else to account, but the only person that benefits from *you* doing your bit is *you*.

It's easy to lie. Who's going to check your working? Hardly anyone.

But!

When you look into the mirror at night, make sure that you're looking into the eyes of an honest ~~monster~~ human. You deserve all the success in the world.

One additional note to bear in mind, you may hear of a lot of writers bragging about their lofty goals and their god-like word counts. Be sure that you don't fall victim to comparisonitis in these situations. You can only do the best you can do, and you never truly know who's telling the truth or who's saying things just to fill their own sails with stinky liar wind.

Pros

- Can give you the boost you so desperately need
- Relatively easy to find accountability partners

- No limit to the number of partners you have
- There are a whole host of groups and communities designed to hold you to account

Cons

- *You* are still in charge of your own success
- Can sometimes be tricky to find *reliable* partners
- Opens yourself up to fall victim to comparisonitis

3.5. IDEATION

As with accountability partners, a collaboration can be something as simple as an ideation session.

You're stuck on the final details of planning your latest story. Your friend is hitting their head against a stone wall wondering how the villain is going to be defeated. You call each other up on the phone and tell each other your woes.

In a bliss-bathing-rising-swell-tide-of-cosmic-fantasm, the magic happens.

We've all heard the expression before: two heads are better than one. Well, that's nearly always the case.

Not only will talking the story out with your ideation partner of choice help clear your head so you can finally secure the closing details of your story, but you may also find that the whole story improves. You go down rabbit holes and tangents looking for the finer details, and with your partner's input, you go to places you never would have gone by yourself.

When working on a story by yourself, you lack two things. Perspective and honest feedback. Often, it's easy to assume that your story is amazing and makes complete sense, because it does to you. You created it.

But when you run the ideas past other people, you may discover that the real clincher of a reason that your protagonist sets forth on her journey of misery, woe and discovery, just doesn't make logical sense. Not only that, but the climax you planned where the protagonist and that antagonist face off toward the end, just comes from out of nowhere and doesn't deliver the message you're wanting it to.

It's better to get feedback early from partners, rather than wait until you've written the story and you hear the mistakes from your ARC team or, worse, your readers when it's published.

Every step made to cement a solid story in the early stages will save you time and heartache later down the line (coincidentally, that's exactly how we'll approach finding and working with your collaborative partner in the next few sections). And that's advice that's coming from me, a pantser by nature. I do very basic plots and pants the rest, but I always make sure the skeleton of my overarching points is solid and in place before I begin any work.

There are a few caveats, here. Firstly, if you are looking for an ideation partner, your chemistry-obsessed sister may not be the best person to give you story ideas for your post-apocalyptic romance. Find people who are working in the same genres, who know the genre conventions that you must adhere to and use *them*. Sure, everyone has ideas, but some people are definitely better equipped to help you please your readers and tick all the boxes of their genre expectations.

Pros

- Fresh new perspectives on story ideas
- Immediate feedback at the planning stage
- A lot of fun, with little commitment on either side

- Relatively easy to find a willing partner
- Save yourself time in veering off-track and re-writing later

Cons

- If you use the wrong partner, their feedback could send you totally off course
- You can get wrapped up in too many tangents and lose yourself in finer details

3.6. ANTHOLOGIES AND BOX SETS

Whoever thought of pooling dozens of short works from authors together in curated anthologies was a genius. For those of you unsure of the difference between anthologies and box sets, it's as simple as the following:

- An **anthology** is a single collection in which individual short stories or novellas have been written specifically (in most cases) for the purpose of being included in a gathered volume of text, from a number of different authors.
- A **box set** is a collection of (often) already published, full-length novels or novellas compiled into one mega volume for the purposes of promotions and sales.

Starting to see where collaboration fits into this? Me too.

Anthologies offer writers the chance to submit smaller works into a collection. As a contributing writer, this could be a fantastic entry point to work on something small with a collaborator. Write your short story, enter the competition and, hopefully, get yourself published. For the person putting the box set together, you have opened yourself up to an opportunity of working directly with a number of fantastic writers as you champion their works and compile them for sale.

Most anthologies by independents will feature a story from the editor of the collection. Anthologies give you a chance to showcase other writers in your genre, while also forging connections with those writers, and compiling all the marketing and promotional savvy of contributing writers so that you may make a collective effort to push yourselves up the chart rankings.

Anthologies are great for widening your audience and showcasing your work to others in your genre, though they can also be a lot of work, too.

If you are the curator of the anthology, you're in for a wild ride. Managing an anthology is a noble task and requires a certain amount of administrative expertise. Not only do you have to open submissions for your anthology (once you've chosen the theme and been very specific to your potential contributors about the requirements of entry to your collection), you also have to read and judge the stories, manage the rejections of those who have missed out on the collection, ensure that you are paying people fairly and have set up clear rewards for those who contribute, and make sure that you're answering any questions along the way.

And that's before you've even narrowed down to your finalists.

Once the final stories have been chosen, you now have the added pressure of knowing that your selected writers are waiting on constant, clear communication from you about every step of the journey. You have to determine the cover art (if you haven't already), you have to deal with the pain of unifying stories and managing edits, while being transparent to writers about any changes that may have been made, all the while answering queries and sorting out launch plans along the way.

Once the product is launched, you've then got to manage the financial aspects (if you've promised royalties), as well as making sure your artists are promoting the book and readers are reviewing. In essence, you're not just promoting the book for yourself, you're promoting the book for all the writers, too. Your reputation hangs on the line, after all!

Still, as much work as all of this is, there is something rewarding to putting anthologies together. When anthologies go smoothly, often you can increase your overall rankings, as well as know that you've made strong author connections. Oftentimes, these collections can be put together rather quickly, and with little need to write too many words yourself, if you're not one who much enjoys the process of lengthy novel-writing.

As for box sets, there are a lot of similarities, though only slightly less work. With box sets, each author is responsible for their edits as each work stands on its own, without the collection. Usually, these are sorted out among authors in tight-knit groups without the need of opening up the works to public submissions, and because of that, these can set in motion rather rapidly.

The main difficulty with box sets is that while anthologies, for the most part, do not sell as well as mainline works, box sets often do. With box sets featuring various authors, someone will have to take the reins with managing and distributing the finances each month and, for some, that can be enough to keep you at arm's reach from this kind of promotion.

Pros

- Great way to connect and network with other writers

- Create some really unique products
- Chance to feature other writers and be responsible for their success
- Writers working together to boost promotion and sales

Cons

- Administration-heavy
- Responsible for royalty-sharing
- Can be hit and miss with sales
- You have to deliver rejection to hopeful contributors who don't make the cut

3.7. THE MELTING POT OF COLLABORATION

I magine yourself a witch and picture your collaborations bottled in dust-layered glass jars. A warped shelf lines the long, stained wall, concealed by a thick cloud of luminescent vapour.

In the centre of the room stands your cauldron. Your own unique brand of collaboration will come to fruition among the bursting boils of thick gelatinous liquid. You select carefully and choose your ingredients with the patient eye of a studious apprentice and, before long, your collaboration is born from the vile stench of wonder before you.

Your collaboration is unique. No one before you, and no one after you will bring your own special flavour to a collaboration. We've spoken about a few of the main collaborations out there, but there is no limit to what you dive into, and how many you choose to undertake. Your threshold for teamwork may be different to others. You may choose to dip your toe into the ocean, and that is fine and okay for you. You are at the helm, and it is upon you to choose what is best for you, no matter what level of collaboration you're involving yourself in.

Me? I like to dabble in a little bit of everything.

You? Who knows?

That's a trick question: *you* do.

Whether you're jumping in 50:50 with another writer on a single book, whether you're joining 50:50 in union by launching a publishing house, whether you're on the phone chatting to a friend about your story ideas, writing under someone else's name, holding someone to account, or opening up your universes for others to play in, the message is clear, and the message is loud.

We're all in this together.

There is no best place to start, and you may find wholly new ways to collaborate with one another. The melting pot can withstand nearly every combination of ingredients and deliver something of value to you. Play a little, experiment, and find the things that work for you.

You may be surprised what you discover about yourself.

3.8. SUMMARY

- **Types of collaboration.** While most people thing of collaboration as simply "co-writing", there are a number of variants that you can explore when looking at collaborating with a partner.
- **Co-writing.** Co-writing exists when two authors stick their hands in the mud and get their selves messy. Traditionally, this can be a 50:50 relationship, but it can deviate from this model.
- **One-offs:** When two (or more) authors write a single story
- **Shared worlds:** When an author shares their universe and characters with other authors, retaining their IP rights to their creation
- **Playing in someone else's sandpit:** When an author writes in someone else's worlds, taking advantage of their reader base, characters, and existing world
- **Publishing partnerships.** An expert-level collaboration in which two authors join together to

form a publishing company. While their roles within the company may vary, each author is legally responsible for the company's success, and each individual contribution counts towards the company's collective success.

- **Ghostwriting.** For the ghostwriter, this is often writing words that will be published in another author's name in return for instant payment. For the person hiring the ghostwriter, this is a great way to meet the demand of a hungry audience and putting out more content. The client must pay well for a good ghostwriter.
- **Accountability partners.** Putting aside the constraints of coordinating worlds and projects, accountability partners are simply other authors who check in with you to ensure that you're meeting your deadlines that you've set. These can be friends, family, writers, or even a number of online services dedicated to holding you to account.
- **Ideation.** Ideation partners are there to support and help you think through your plot lines and narrative blocks. It could be as simple as a friendly ear you can borrow on the phone, or as complex as monthly ideation meetings with a white board involved.
- **Anthologies and box sets.** A great way to reach more readers and network with other authors, anthologies and multi-author box sets are an innovative way to repurpose content and dip your toe in the collaboration arena as you combine your marketing efforts.
- **The melting pot of collaboration.** There is no one way to collaborate. Collaborations are individual,

unique, and you can never have the same collaboration twice. There is no limit to how many collaborations you want to involve yourself in, just make sure you don't overload yourself or pick up too much too quickly.

COLLABORATION CASE STUDY: ANGELINE TREVENA AND H.B. LYNE

Angeline Trevena and H.B. (Holly) Lyne are the power duo behind the *Unstoppable Authors* podcast and the masterminds behind the UK's Indie Fire Writers Conference. They each write across the science fiction and fantasy genres, and I'd be doing a disservice if I didn't give each of them a highlight from their respective bios.

Angeline Trevena is a British science fiction, fantasy and horror author. She's been writing stories since she was old enough to hold a pen, and after gaining a BA Hons degree in Drama and Writing, she honed her craft with horror and fantasy shorts which are published in numerous magazines and anthologies.

H.B. Lyne has always lived close to the dark side, never quite mastering the ability to force choke but contemplating it during dark times. These days, when not chasing two chaotic munchkins around, Holly somehow engineers time to write fantasy.

Together, Angeline and Holly act as accountability partners for each other and are in the process of laying the foundations of creating a shared world within which they will each write individual stories.

DAN: How did you two first begin collaborating?

ANGELINE: Myself and Holly met one another in a Facebook group for authors, and I think we hit it off because we write in similar genres and have quite similar lives and goals.

We then met in person at a convention, and, quite independently, we both came up with the idea that we wanted to do some sort of collaborative project together. I had started a podcast some time before, but let it languish by the wayside, and we both decided that it would be great to pick it up again as a project together. Since then, we've built a world together, and we'll both be writing novellas set in that world.

DAN: What qualities do you look for in a collaborator?

H.B.: Complementary goals, strengths. The ability to get along and be adaptable, while being at a similar stage of our careers.

ANGELINE: I'm very indecisive, so I need a collaborator who can push through decisions and stop me dithering. I need someone who's down-to-earth and realistic. Also, it's really handy to have a collaborator who can empathize with my time and commitment pressures and restrictions. I'm a full-time mum to two young children, and they will always be my priority. I need to work with someone who can understand that, and knows that, sometimes, I'll have to drop the ball for family commitments.

DAN: HAVE YOU EVER SAID "NO" to a potential collaborator?

ANGELINE: I have, simply because my gut told me to. It's so important to trust your gut, and to remember that, however good friends you might be with someone, you might not work well together.

DAN: How has your collaboration affected your individual work?

H.B.: It's improved it. Although it is challenging to fit everything in, having the accountability helps enormously.

ANGELINE: One really important thing it's done, is to teach me to let go of control a little, in a really good way. I'm a bit of a micro-manager, and I can sometimes get really closed down to other people's approaches, preferring to do things my way or not at all. Also, with Holly and I acting as accountability partners, she has made me more organized, less of a procrastinator, a better prioritizer, and more decisive (possibly!)

DAN: What is something that you hear a lot about collaboration that just isn't true?

. . .

ANGELINE: That it makes or breaks a friendship. Sure, collaborating absolutely can break friendships, but it's not some kind of test. It's a part of a friendship, or a shift in one. Just like any relationship, it needs constant work and adjustment. There will be compromise, and give and take, and it's a constant aspect that changes and fluctuates, one that's dynamic.

It's not a case that, if you collaborate on a project, you'll either never speak again or your future collaborations will be perfect. There's no perfect relationship, and they change day by day. Switching to becoming partners on a work project will change aspects of your friendship, but it doesn't rewrite the whole thing. It's merely one part of your ongoing, ever-changing relationship.

DAN: How have you tackled any situations where the collaboration was in jeopardy or didn't match your expectations?

ANGELINE: No collaboration is ever going to be perfect, and it's really important to take things one day at a time. You both need to be willing to pick up the other's slack when they have other things going on.

We all know that "life happens", and you need to be ready to step in and prop the project up while your partner deals with whatever else they have going on. But, it's important to remember that it needs to be give and take. If one person is doing all the giving, it might be time to call it a day.

Also, communication is key. If you seethe in private, it's just going to build up resentment. If there's an issue, you need to talk to your partner about it, and give yourselves a chance to fix it. Don't split up a collaboration for an issue you didn't even give your partner the opportunity to resolve.

. . .

DAN: How much importance do you place on contracts and agreements in a collaborative project?

H.B.: So far trust has been fine for us, but I do think contracts are a good idea when it comes to money.

ANGELINE: I think they are important, but I'm not sure they always need to be sealed with blood, signed on the dotted line, or witnessed by a judge. A more casual agreement can work too. Of course, it entirely depends on the kind of relationship you have, and it's important to remember that any relationship can turn sour, however solid you think it might be.

DAN: What, in your opinion, are the main benefits of collaboration?

ANGELINE: So many! Having someone whose strengths match your weaknesses, and vice versa. Holly and I definitely make one another better! Having an outside eye on your ideas and having an extra brain to brainstorm with. We can pool our resources, our networks, and connections. We can be one another's wingman. We can be each other's cheerleader. Plus, this whole authoring business can get really lonely, so it's great to have someone to bounce ideas off, to empathize with you, and to just chat with.

. . .

H.B.: Accountability, having a partner to bounce ideas off and pooling time and resources.

DAN: Are there any softwares or systems that are fundamental to your collaboration?

ANGELINE: We've used a few different apps and systems, but the ones we've stuck with throughout are Google Docs, where absolutely everything gets saved so that we both have access to it, and Discord, where we can text, voice, and video chat, as well as share documents.

H.B.: Trello for planning. MailerLite allows multiple users with customizable levels of access, which is very handy for mailing list management.

DAN: What one piece of advice would you give to someone looking to get involved in their first collaborative project?

H.B.: Get to know the other person well first. Make sure you're on the same page and get along well.

ANGELINE: Trust your gut. Nothing is more important. While you should always be open to changing your mind about someone, trust your instincts.

PART IV

FINDING YOUR COLLABORATOR

4. FINDING YOUR COLLABORATOR

Collaborators can be found in a number of places. On message boards, in writer's groups, on social media, through friends and recommendations.

There is no one place to find a collaborator, as there is no right place to find your perfect romantic partner in life. Collaboration is a game of numbers and exploration, and only then will you be able to find someone that works for you.

Let's explore this notion of "perfect". A *perfect* partner. If you are looking for someone to accompany you on a frictionless breeze through the streets of collab, who will throw rose petals at your feet while constantly reminding you that you look amazing and that "Ooh, damn, your efforts in the gym are really paying off", then maybe you need to remove those rose-tinted glasses and lower your expectations.

There is no perfect partner. Everyone has their flaws, and everyone has their baggage. Have you been approached by someone to collaborate and you've thought, "you're not quite at my level, kid, I need someone to boost me higher, not drag me down?"

Then you're looking at it all wrong.

Put aside any pretence of knowing exactly who you're looking for and open your eyes to possibility. Do you know someone who complains constantly that they hate first drafting? Do you know someone who excels in marketing but lacks the funding to put a project together? Have you come across someone literally shouting, *"Hey! I'm looking for a collaborator for my space robot end-of-the-world erotica western!"*?

Your first collaboration might not be exactly what you were looking for, but it might be exactly what you need. Identify the areas of opportunity or want and find a place where you fit in. What do *you* want out of this?

Need (or) Want + Opportunity = Collaboration

Make a list

Once you've identified the need or want that you would like to fill, then you can start identifying a list of people who might fit that bill. Write them down. Be crass and rank them in order of preference. Remember, you have a reason for wanting to make this happen.

See if you can identify at least 20 people who you'd like to collaborate with. Fill up a sheet with their names and try to find their contact information (assume I'm advising you use the legal route to obtain this). Soon we're going to reach out and start asking.

But, don't worry. Not yet. The next thing we need to do is...

4.1. IDENTIFY WHAT YOU CAN BRING TO THE TABLE

You've got your list of 20 people, and already your heart is a fluttering moth in a bird cage. Slow down, cowpoke, we've got more work to do.

Take a look at each of those names on your list. Each one of those men and women have vastly unique lives. Every one of them is an individual with their own hopes and dreams, their own set of financial circumstances, their own responsibilities and dependents, their own families and friends, their own habits and routines, their own world views and opinions.

I've seen a lot of people offer blanket templates to contact individuals, not just with collaboration, but with a myriad of things. After years of working within communications and marketing and having been approached on several occasions by potential collaborators who clearly hadn't done their research, the biggest lesson I've learned is that **you must individualize each letter, text, email or call.**

Before you throw this book on the table, run off and grab your copy of *The Order of the Phoenix* instead, know that I'm not suggesting you painstakingly write 20 individual letters, with no familiarities at all. I'm saying that the key to successful first point contact is personalization. Remember, in some cases, this could be your first and only chance to make a good first impression.

But we'll get to that shortly.

For now, I want you to focus on each name *individually*. You have chosen these people specifically, but do you know why you chose them?

- Maybe you chose Abi because she's killing it in the romance genre, and you think she could raise your status as a romance writer
- Perhaps you selected John because he's already collaborating with a dozen authors and he might be an easy win
- Or maybe you've chosen Susan because you *love* her writing, but think she's massively under-appreciated by her fans

Look carefully at your list and write down three reasons that outline why you want to work with them. Be explicit, no one is going to see this list except for you. Adhere to all the rules in Chapter 2 of this book. Now's the time to be honest and set your ego aside.

Once you've chosen your three reasons you want to work with these collaborators, you're going to want to think *reeeally* hard about what exactly it is that *you* can bring to the table.

The number one mistake authors make in finding a collaborator is looking at the collaboration from only their own point of view. Seeing what it can do for *them*.

I cannot stress this enough. You're soon going to be reaching out and asking these people to devote their time to you, to put their trust in you and create a partnership that transcends the notion of the typical author's life. When you do, you're going to want to make damn sure that you've got a compelling reason as to why they should even consider you as a partner.

We'll go into examples of communications in the following sections, "The wrong way" and "The right way", but for now, focus on that list and get jotting down three key reasons your potential collaborator might want to consider joining forces with you.

Example 1: An established writer

Name: Jerry Donavan
Reasons why *I* want to collaborate:

- I'm a big fan of his work
- He's got a big audience and that could help me
- He seems really down-to-earth and accessible online

Things that I bring to the table:

- I'm a fast writer
- I know his works already, so would be a handy asset to write with
- I've got a track record of delivering projects when I plan to

Example 2: A close writer friend

Name: Kerry Leedswick
Reasons why *I* want to collaborate:

- We're already great friends and we're on the same step of our author journey
- She writes in my genre and is *killing* it on Kobo, while I'm not
- We see a lot of each other already, I know we're compatible people

Things that I bring to the table:

- I'm killing it on Amazon, whereas she isn't
- I live across the road so we can physically meet and hold each other to account
- I'm great at first drafts, while I know that she hates them

IN THE NEXT SECTION, we're going to look at breaking the ice and reaching out to the people on our list of desirable collaborators. Scary stuff, huh?

It doesn't have to be, as long as we cover all bases. In the pages ahead, I'm going to take you through the right and the wrong ways to approach your future collaborator, so that you can take that confident first step on your collaboration journey.

But first, we're going to find out why collaborators say "no", so you can learn from the mistakes of those who came before.

4.2. THE WRONG WAY

There are a thousand ways to screw up a first impression.

First impressions are made within the first seven seconds of any interaction. Whether that's meeting someone face-to-face or asking them to read your email.

First impressions count. For many potential collaborations, you will not get a second chance to ask again. That may seem like a lot of pressure, because it is. If you've got your hopes and dreams set out on working with Stephen King and becoming his next collaborator (which, I'm sorry to say, *is* highly unlikely, but not impossible) then you better be sure you're saying the right things and appeasing the right desires from your future collaborative partner.

Things go wrong when we don't look at the opportunity from the other person's perspective. As outlined in the previous pages, you need to play to *their* wants and needs, rather than your own. There needs to be a genuine connection. Don't just eyeball a stranger and do your best to fumble through and fake authenticity. People can sniff that shit a mile away. "I can tell when people don't know me very well, because they just glanced over something that they could find on the Amazon author page, and then they just get right into their pitch," says J. Thorn.

Here are a couple of examples of how to send an email that will guarantee you a "no".

Example 1. Short and sour

 Hey,

I didn't know if you were looking for any collaborators, but I love what you're doing and think we'd make a great team! Hit me up if you want to talk more.

Dan

Sigh...

Where's the substance? Where's the connection? Where's the heart?

As someone who has received my fair share of invitations to collaborate, this one would instantly get rejected. There's no context, no indicator that this would in any way be a good idea for us to collaborate. This is the equivalent of performing a collaboration drive-by, leaning out of the window and hurling a screwed-up note onto my front garden as you scream, "Thanks for your consideration!" I can tell that I'm just one among a hundred people you sent this blanket message to, and to be perfectly frank, I don't care for it.

Example 2. Butter me up, buttercup

 Yo!

I absolutely LOVE your work and I've seen that you collaborate with other authors on your books. I'm in the market for collaboration and I'd LOVE the chance to work with you.

I'm such a big fan of your *Guardians of the Universe* series. A cyber-western set in space? That's such a cool concept! I couldn't put the damn thing down for days! When's the next book coming out?

Anyway, I've got this great idea, where Serena and Troy explore a subsection of the universe in which a planet is covered in a tropical jungle, but all the bugs are as big as elephants and all the elephants are as big as cats. We could add some cool space pirates and really blow this universe wide open.

Hit me back and let me know!

Dan

Mouth flaps open and closed

How would you react if you opened an email and read this? While there may be more substance, the entire email is one-sided. It's always nice to hear from one of your fans, but where's the specificity in the email? Let's imagine that Serena and Troy are mentioned in all of the blurbs for this imaginary series. Let's assume that there's already a pre-order page live for book seven. Does that change how you read this email?

And, even if the sender of this email *is* a fan and *has* read your books, would you appreciate someone diving in with their version of what a story might look like before you've even had a chance to say "Hello?" Probably not.

By all means flatter, but there is a way to do this with class. You *do* want to tug at your potential collaborators ego and get them interested in your pitch, but dear God take things slowly and be more delicate in your approach. Have you ever tried to pull someone on a night out by clutching their arm, whirling them to face you (spilling their Martini along the way), and bellowing how much you love what they're working with?

It rarely ever works.

There's also the small matter of the fact that there's no real pull as to *why* they should consider working with you. What's in it for your collaborator? Why should they bother? What can you bring to the table?

This would be another email I'd reply with a simple, "Thanks, but no thanks." I'm a busy guy. I don't want to waste time going down the rabbit hole of investigating *you* when I've already got a thousand things going on. Remember, asking someone to collaborate is a big deal. It takes a lot of energy and effort, and unless you can hook someone in the right way, they're likely going to say no immediately.

Unless, of course, you have some kind of previous relationship with this person and they know enough about you to open up to the consideration. Still, it works to be kind and show why it would be advantageous for both.

4.3. THE RIGHT WAY

Truth be told, as there are a thousand ways to screw this up, there are also a thousand ways to maximize your chances for success.

That's what we're doing, here. Ensuring that you are giving yourself the *best* chance of making the magic happen. I do not promise a magic formula that works for everyone, but what I can do is give you methods which increase your odds and put you on the path to success.

Remember that list you made of reasons why you want to work with these individuals? You won't be using those, but they're useful to keep in mind.

Remember the reasons that your prospective collaborator will benefit from working with you?

This is where all those pieces of the puzzle come together, in your carefully scripted, well-crafted email. Please bear in mind that I don't recommend copying and pasting these emails verbatim. These are examples highlighting key points. I recommend you take the time to craft your own versions of these emails using the principles I lay out ahead.

First, we'll look at proposing the idea to someone who you

haven't had too many encounters with. You couldn't call them a friend, but you could potentially call them an acquaintance.

The cold call

For the purposes of this message, let's assume that you've never spoken to this author before. You're contacting from out of the blue. You're familiar with this author's work, and you genuinely feel you can add some value to their writing life. How might we go about establishing a connection, and delivering the ask?

 (1) Hi [name],

(2) I came across your work while researching for my latest novel, and I'm a big fan of what you're doing within the author space. I devoured [book] in a few days and your work reminds me a lot of my recent project [book].

(3) Given that we both work within pretty similar arenas, I wondered if there was a potential here to look at a collaboration together? I'm known as a fast, quality writer, with a slew of reviews that back up the quality of the works I produce. By working together, we could potentially produce a novel that would be published much quicker than by working on our own individual works, while also delivering to wider audience bases.

(4) By all means, take some time to consider this. I've always been told that "if you don't ask, the answer is always *no*." I'd love to have the chance to

work with you and am happy to discuss this further if you have any questions. If you'd like to see examples of my work, I'm happy to provide some of those, too.

(5) If you're not interested, that's not a problem at all, and I wish you the best with your writing career.

[6] Thankfully,

[Name]

THE EMAIL IS SIMPLE, it's clear, it's direct. You want your prospective collaborator to know exactly what you're asking upfront, but you also don't want to get bogged down in details.

At this point, you want to just tempt your collaborator. Float the idea. You're extending an offer, but it's inside a sealed envelope. That doesn't mean you're tricking them, what it does do is causes intrigue, while not wasting their time. An email like this is respectful. It's professional. It flatters, while also allowing you to promote your own skills so they can see the benefits of working with you. It's short enough that you're not wasting someone's time by reading it.

As I've said already, there's no set formula. However, we can break the above email into a few key sections. I'd also like to restate at this point, that the idea of this is not to copy and paste the email and then canvas 300 messages by throwing addresses into a BCC line (or, worse, accidentally putting 300 email addresses in the CC line—*barf!*), but it's to illustrate *one* approach.

1. The introduction

Keep it simple. Keep it relatively casual, and within limits of a normal conversation. "Yo!" or "Hey!" are too casual for a cold call. "Dearest" and "To whom it may concern," are too formal. Find the balance. "Hello" and "Hi" are classics. They do just fine, here.

Also bear in mind any particular preferred names. Some writers go by abbreviated names on podcasts (most of the time, I'm known as Dan, but my pen name is Daniel). Go with the author's pen name for safety. You're not best buddies with them, you're engaging in a professional relationship. Maybe the Daves, Matts, and Sues will come, but until then, go with their full name.

(Bonus tip, if your prospective collaborator *does* reply, then take a look at what they call themselves at the bottom of the email. That's your way forward from then on out).

2. Flatter and connect

We've spoken about how too much flattery can be a bad thing. When I say "flatter", I'm not proposing that you dive in with disingenuous chat-up lines or run your mouth with a list of things that you *think* they will want to hear.

People can smell fake a mile away. Even in text form, it's easy to tell who genuinely appreciates your work, and who's blowing smoke up your ass in the hopes of taking advantage of your generous nature.

Be honest. Be genuine. You don't want to start the relationship off with deceit, nor feel like you're immediately setting the collaboration off-balance. Find a common ground between the pair of you and find a few nice things to say. I'm assuming you've already seen enough of their stuff to know that you're a good match together, otherwise, why the hell are you reaching out to them?

Notice here that I don't also immediately start with the demand for a consideration for collaboration. I ease into it. I make a connection. Remember the human in the bar whose arm you grabbed and screamed in their face? Would you continue shouting, telling them about how eager you are to build a life together? No. Hopefully not, anyway. Establish a connection, and then continue.

3. Establish and show your working

You've pulled them in. You've got their attention. Now it's time to get to the point.

Take your time crafting this section. It may yet be the most important of all.

There's a balance to be struck here between abrasive and woolly. You don't want to demand the collaboration, but neither do you want to beat around the bush. You're establishing that you're open to the possibility, and then you're listing why you believe this to be true.

This is the turning point between when someone who is interested will read on, and someone who isn't interested will simply close the window or offer a brief reply of "no thanks". Section (2) of the email increases your chances of further readthrough because you're establishing the emotional connection that will trigger your potential collaboration. What happens after that, is up to them.

Keep it brief. List your points and move on. Writers don't want you gushing over them for paragraph after paragraph (okay, maybe some do), but it doesn't benefit you. Remember all that stuff about "knowing your worth", and getting used to "no"? This is where all of that comes into practice.

Be bold but be humble. If you genuinely believe this collaboration could work, you are on equal footing with the person you're reaching out to. You're offering them something amazing, whether they take it or not is up to them.

This might be your bulkiest section of your email, but don't stretch it out. Their time is precious, and so is yours. Get to the point, give them a sniff of bacon (or tofu), and let their salivary glands begin to drool.

4. Soften the severity of the ask

You've stated what you want, you've laid out your reasons, and now it's time to pull back a little.

This might be contrary to what a lot of people advise, but I can safely say that this formula has worked wonders with every collaboration I've entered into. Collaborations are a big ask, it may be likely that your potential partner wasn't even thinking about this, and they're already knee-deep in wrapping up their sixteen-book series, entering shorts to anthologies, and finalizing the particulars of a conference that they're coordinating.

Don't slam the brakes but do ease off the throttle.

The "If you don't ask, the answer is always no", line has worked for me time and time again. Not in a crafty way, but I genuinely believe that advice. You get nowhere if you don't ask, so why not take the plunge? By opening yourself up and acknowledging to the person you're asking that you understand that it's something of a big ask, they're likely going to connect with you more. You've been brave. You've been bold. You've been original. That's something to be admired.

Perhaps they've had situations in the past where they can

place themselves in your shoes in that moment. You've shown humility, that's a trait that can take you *far* in this game.

Not only that, but you've reinforced that you'd love to work with *them*, and that you are open to further discussion. The ball is in their court, figuratively speaking. They have an option to explore further without commitment. You've already opened up the doors to two-way conversation, and that's a pretty big deal.

5. Give them an out

This one comes back to humility.

Nothing makes me feel safer in someone's company, than when I have the option to leave. At parties, I may swan around friendship groups, spilling my whiskey over my thumb and licking it up like a booze-addled Dalmatian, but the only way I'm able to remain confident is because I know I can leave whenever I like.

When there is no clear exit, the walls narrow in. You sit in the corner and check your watch and wait for it all to be over, looking around you for any means of unorthodox escape. The air vents could barely fit a 4-year-old, but maybe if you sucked in your gut and greased yourself up with lard, you could climb through.

By giving your prospective collaborator an out, you're really giving them a larger in. You're saying that you understand that they may not want to invest right now, but the offer is there. You're allowing them the human prerogative of choice. I can't tell you how important this is for me when someone reaches out. Immediately, by someone simply *offering* a suggestion that no is okay, it eases the pressure and, simply, makes me like you more. It highlights humility, it oozes understanding. I like you a little bit more as a human being.

Be honest with yourself. Wouldn't you feel hella happier

saying no to an invite to your best friend's wedding in Vegas, knowing that it's going to cost your entire life savings to go, because they've offered you an out and already told you it's not going to affect your friendship?

Unless your friend's a goddamn liar. I'm looking at you Katherine. No amount of Vanish will ever remove that red wine stain you "accidentally" spilled on my white carpet after you and Tim came back from your honeymoon in Mauritius.

No matter whether you receive a yes or no at this point, one thing will be certain. Anyone who makes it to the end of your email will respond with kind words. A "no" can hurt, but not when it's delivered with kindness and an appreciation for the ask.

6. Signing off

Nice and simple, and sometimes personal to each sender. I always sign off with a "Thankfully" to most of my emails. None of this "Kind regards" rubbish, thank them for their time. "Thankfully" is simple, elegant and a fair notch below other formal substitutes that I grew sick and tired of when working in a corporate environment.

And no "Cheers", either. You're possible writing partners, not chummy pub mates.

Asking a friend

I'm not going to spend a lot of time on this one as I don't know anything about the specifics of you and your friend's relationship.

Maybe you've known each other for years. Maybe you've recently reconnected and realized you work in similar fields.

Maybe you've bumped into each other at a writing group and think you'd be a good fit working together.

Whatever the reason, you're going to have to tailor-make your pitch for these people. The principles above are a great way to start, and they give you a basic skeleton for approaching someone with whom you already have a history. Ease into it, ask without expectation, and give them an out.

If at all possible, ask them in person. Call them on the phone. If you're imagining that Aunt Leah is going to be a great person to collaborate with, or your best friend from ten years ago who you call every third Sunday would benefit from this kind of partnership, then utilize those connections. In-person and phone are a thousand times better than the written word.

Oh, and don't put too much pressure on it. If they're your friend, they'll either accept or let you down with kindness.

If they don't, then find better friends. *Gawd.*

4.4. AFTER YOU CLICK SEND

Take a breather.

Wait for your hands to stop shaking.

Have a cup of tea.

Carry on.

Once the message has been sent out into the intersphere, there's little more you can do. Sure, it might be daunting knowing that somewhere, someone is reading your strange little request and judging your words and whether or not you're worth considering, but none of that is up to you, now.

In the famous words of one great grey wizard, "All we have to decide is what to do with the time that is given to *us*."

I don't know you from Adam. Maybe you find certain things harder to let go than others do, but I can promise you that, whatever comes next, you're equipped to handle it.

Remember that section on "No?" That's where your ability to take whatever comes to you is put to the test.

The reality is that things don't always go our way. Sometimes people are busy, and we unknowingly reach out to them at an awkward time. Sometimes life happens, sometimes pipes break and put us in a foul mood, sometimes our children spill milk on the seats of a brand-new car, sometimes, sometimes people are so overwhelmed by their full-time job that they don't have any headspace to consider letting anyone else in. Sometimes people just don't answer in the way you expect them to.

Your answer might be a no. But, it also might be a yes. Why worry about it until you receive that fateful email that either launches you on your springboard or sends you back to the drawing board.

And maybe you're left waiting for an hour before you get your reply. Maybe you're left waiting for 3 weeks. What are you going to do in the time that you're left waiting for a response?

Carry on. Write some words. Send a few more emails. What harm can it possibly do?

There's something magical about playing the numbers game. It's the same as writing. When you first put finger to keyboard and start scripting your first story, every moment is precious. You savour each word and you smell each paragraph. You lose yourself in the eddies of the chapters and follow the current towards the finish line.

You hit publish.

You celebrate.

You start the process all over again.

The more you write, the easier it gets. It's the same with this process. You may have your heart fixed on collaborating with one person, but that's not the end of this journey. They may just say no, and for that you will be thankful.

I've said it before, and I'll say it again: a person who says no is doing you a favour. You don't want to work with someone whose heart and soul isn't truly invested in your project.

And remember, while there may be a lot of "no's", sooner or later, you will also get a "yes".

4.5. AFTER THE YES

When a yes finally does come in, you may find that you suffer from at least one or all of the following symptoms:

- Excitement
- An impulse to engage in alcoholic consumption
- Heart palpitations
- Both a dry and over-salivating mouth
- Squeals
- Knocking over your gin and tonic in a fit of ecstasy
- A sudden, all-encompassing realization that this is actually happening and you didn't actually think beyond the initial email sending so what the hell are you supposed to do now this woman is a pretty big deal and she's taking a chance on me and wants to work with me and what if I screw it up but what if it's the best thing that ever happened I'm not prepared there's so much that could go wrong and work's already kicking my keister and there are a—

Stop.

Breathe.

I've been there. I've been blessed with a "yes" from a top-ranking Amazon author who wanted to work with me. I punched the ceiling and made holes. My heart fluttered more in those proceeding 10 minutes than it did when I experienced my first pregnancy scare. It can be a big deal, and yes, it's going to happen. Your project has legs.

Your collaboration may simply be a "yes" from a close friend as opposed to a stranger, but the emotions still apply. You're setting out on a brand-new adventure, and that can be both terrifying and exciting. Your next few interactions with your fellow collaborator are going to be key, and it is in these meetings and discussions that you lay the foundation for how you are going to work together, and the roles and responsibilities you take as partners.

But first, take a moment to celebrate.

You started something today.

You're setting forth on your adventure.

Kick back, celebrate with your loved ones, and get a good night's rest.

The hard work starts tomorrow.

4.6. SUMMARY

- **Finding your collaborator.** Collaborators can be found in a number of places. Within your friendship groups, in online communities, through reaching out on the internet with strangers who you feel would be suitable.

ACTION: Think about who you want to collaborate with and make a list of at least 20 possible collaboration partners.

- **Identifying what you can bring to the table.** Know your worth and think up reasons why *they* would want to work with *you*. It's easier to say why you want to work with them but remember you're trying to hook human beings into working closely with you for an extended period of time.

ACTION: Write three things you can bring to the table as well as three reasons why you want to work with each collaborator.

- **The wrong way.** You only get one chance at a first

impression and there are a thousand ways to cock up the intro and the pitch. Review the chapter to find the examples of poor introductions and pitches.

- **The right way.** Be human, be professional, give them a chance to say no. Breathe, don't put too much pressure on yourself and show your authenticity. Be humble. Review the chapter for an example of a good first pitch.
- **After you click send.** Relax, don't overthink it, and move on to the next one. The ball is no longer in your court. Don't rush your potential collaborator and continue with your work until their response comes. If it's a no, then hold that chin high and try your next candidate.
- **After the yes.** Celebrate, share in your joy with your loved ones, sleep. When you wake up, it's time to begin the hard work.

COLLABORATION CASE STUDY: MICHAEL ANDERLE

M ichael Anderle is the Amazon best-selling author of over 27 series, 4 story universes, and 160 audio books, of which all of these have been published by his independent publishing company, LMBPN, in the last 3 years.

His leading series, *The Kurtherian Gambit*, houses almost 200 books, with collaborations from a multitude of best-selling and leading independent authors, and spans across several genres including; science-fiction, space opera, fantasy, and post-apocalyptic. His Facebook group, 20Booksto50K®, is now one of the leading pages for independent writers to share knowledge and ask questions, with the group hosting over 40,000 members at the time of publication.

When it comes to collaboration, I could think of nobody better to talk to than someone who has collaborated in virtually every single way. Michael's collaborations take a variety of forms and cover almost everything discussed in this book. I've had the pleasure of collaborating with Michael on several works for his *Kurtherian Gambit* universe and have seen first-hand just how intricate his network of writers is. The following interview is just a small glimpse inside the mind of one of the most fertile and practised independent collaborators in the game today.

DAN: How did you first begin collaborating?

MICHAEL: My fans wanted more stories than I could possibly write in any material amount of time. So, the option was to either *not* provide stories fans would want or collaborate.

DAN: What qualities do you look for in a collaborator?

MICHAEL: Personality, professionalism, punctuality, performance.

DAN: Have you ever said no to a potential collaborator? If so, why?

MICHAEL: Yes, because it wasn't a collaboration. It was a, "I have this great idea, and why don't you handle it so we get a lot of money, I just know it will be big."

DAN: How has your collaboration impacted your work?

MICHAEL: Collaborations bring a great opportunity to expand the thinking up and refining of a concept. Both (or more) of the collaborators have ideas which (can) help the flavour of the final product.

For example, I've had situations where my original idea was solid, they came in from a different angle and, the next thing I know, I'm off dreaming up a tangential concept I *never* would have thought of without their suggestions.

The new idea was good, the final idea was superior.

Sometimes, it's only a tweak to a character's personality that can help them become a beloved character. The tweak is usually something very personal to the collaborator, fleshing out a new reality to the characters I would not have been able to do.

Why? I had no personal experience to even dream it up.

DAN: What is something that you often hear about collaboration that just isn't true?

MICHAEL: It's easy and stress-free. More words, half the effort. It's going to be rainbows and unicorns or something along those lines.

Collaborations can be a lot of fun, but stress-free (or ego-free) is usually not one of them.

DAN: How have you tackled any situations where the collaboration was in jeopardy or didn't match your expectations?

MICHAEL: The ones that stick out are when two collaborators are very opinionated. Usually, it can be from those who have less experience wanting exactly what they would do if they were solo.

If you expect to have it only one way, why is this a collaboration?

If it is one way that is a mentorship with credit.

DAN: How important are contracts and agreements to a collaborative project?

MICHAEL: Unfortunately, the agreements are necessary. The more we do collaborations, the more I'm hammered by the [legal] ramifications of a handshake agreement. I'm from Texas, I'm still having to learn why handshake agreements aren't a good idea.

Further, I have to learn that lawyers aren't evil and negotiations during the process don't have to be stressful.

DAN: What, for you, are the main benefits of collaboration?

MICHAEL: Anyone who knows me has heard that my mountain (my goal) is to create stories that fans want to re-read and make an income.

Collaborations work to attain that goal.

DAN: Are there any softwares or systems that are fundamental to your collaboration?

MICHAEL: We use Abacus (by PublishDrive) to run our accounting splits, Google Docs for shared information, and

Slack for communication (also to share Word Documents if Google Docs isn't a choice). We use Zoom for conference calls.

DAN: What one piece of advice would you give to someone looking to get involved in their first collaborative project?

MICHAEL: What are you bringing to the collaboration? Know your why and make sure that the person you are collaborating with will take it as seriously as you do.

If you have a volatile life, consider putting off the collaboration if you can't make your due dates.

PART V

LAYING THE FOUNDATIONS

5. LAYING THE FOUNDATIONS

The Empire State Building would be nothing without a strong foundation.

I mean, can you imagine the sheer architectural genius that has been poured into the design of that building to ensure that it doesn't just wilt like my sister's sunflowers and kiss the ground?

Foundations are *everything*. Your collaborative foundations are no exception.

Now that you've got your collaborative partner, it's time to set the stage. Maybe you've had a couple of exchanges and answered any hanging questions before they've committed, or possibly they were so eager to work with you that they replied in an instant.

Whatever the situation, before you go sprinting off into the savannah to get to work, you must establish just what exactly your collaboration is going to entail.

This part is difficult for a lot of people, and I can already feel eyes pulling away from the page because, "I already know how it's going to work, we're already so in sync that these are all wasted words, disembodied spirit of Daniel Willcocks..." Well,

before you do skip this section, just humour me for a moment...
Please.

I once heard that any legally binding agreement isn't so much an "agreement" in a positive sense but should be viewed as a "*dis*agreement".

You've just committed to working together. You're excited to get going. But the truth is that neither of you completely know what you're getting into yet. You've not ironed out the specifics, you've not discussed the percentage share of intellectual property, or the financial split should the product excel. You've not even so much as set deadlines for when you're hoping to bring your new book baby into the world.

It all sounds boring, I know, but this is the part where you can save the most time and heartache in the long run. I've learned this mistake the hard way. A blasé attitude will only get you so far. What happens if you create a wildly successful series, and even though you put in all of the hard work, your collaborator steals the IP and runs off into the ether? What happens if *you* thought you'd be published by April, but your collaborator thought you meant the book would be *finished* by April but *published* in July.

Don't be shy of sweating the small stuff. Here, the small stuff matters. Once the glow and excitement of the "yes" has worn off, it's time to get to Business.

Yes, that's Business with a capital B.

Because that's what this is. You've created a Business arrangement with a collaborator, and now it's time to make the magic happen.

Over the next few sections, I've made it my mission to highlight the key things to address and look for when establishing the intricacies of your collaborative relationship, so that you can set forth on the path to success and you can both Rock the Casbah.

5.1. (DIS)AGREEMENTS

I cannot stress this enough: no matter what type of collaboration you enter into, you *must* have some kind of contract.

I also cannot stress this enough: I am a hypocrite. It has only been in the last year or two that I've taken these seriously and, I can guarantee you, it has saved my ass on more than one occasion.

Contracts are the bedrock of your collaboration, yet for some people, contracts are intimidating pieces of paper with lots of words and terminology like "heretofore" and "hereby known as" scattered throughout the document. Contracts are thrown around in court and are used to hold you to account on the things you've promised to do.

Yuck. Who needs that?

However, if we reframe what we're looking at here, we can find a softer way to discuss contracts. Let's heretofore—see what I did there?—relabel "Contracts" as "Agreements".

There. That's better.

I'll be honest, my earliest collaborations still don't have agreements in place. It's something that I'm working on, since I have these in place for my latest partnerships. If I could go back and set them up from the beginning, you'd be damn sure that I would.

 Contracts and agreements for timelines, payment (if applicable), and scope of work are so important. These are a safety net for all parties involved, and they help keep everyone on track while also knowing what's possible and when. It's a fantastic tool for gauging how a first-time collaboration is going to work out.

— KATHRIN HUTSON

Agreements are created so that both of you know *exactly* what's going on and what's expected of you. When creating an agreement, you have the opportunity to declare the things *you need* from the collaboration, and you have a platform to negotiate with your partner on *their needs*. Everything listed in the agreement is explicit, and anything left out of the agreement is inherently then left up for grabs by whoever chooses to argue the loudest if it ever comes to blows.

That's why, as I mentioned, "(Dis)agreements" is a better term for this document. It lays out exactly who gets what in the rare occurrence that you and your partner fall on bad terms and decide to fight for the scraps. If you've neglected to mention you wanted a 50% share in audiobook rights, then it's very possible you may lose these completely if they're not written in your (dis)agreement.

No one likes to think of the bad side of a collaborative effort. Everyone wants to imagine that the partnership will be a breeze and that everything will be smooth sailing. As optimistic as we want to be when entering a collaboration, sadly, sometimes things don't go our way, so it's worth covering yourself in case of emergencies.

Keep it explicit. Keep it clear.

It's been said a thousand times before, but I'll add it again here: clarity is king.

I want to reiterate that *now* is your primary opportunity to ensure that everything that happens with your collaboration is above board and meets your expectations. Don't worry about dragging things out, don't fret about taking time to talk to your significant other, don't worry about asking any questions that you may feel are stupid. Now is your time to be clear about what you're willing to give, and any red lines that you simply do not cross.

This collaboration must work for both of you. Ensure that there are no ambiguous terms or responsibilities before you ignite your rocket fuel and explode your project into the stratosphere.

5.2. THE (DIS)AGREEMENT CHECKLIST

Okay, I feel like this is the most pertinent place to reclaim something that I have mentioned a couple of times already in this book:

IMPORTANT NOTE: Daniel Willcocks is not a legal professional. Sometimes he shouts at the TV during Law & Order, *but his extent of legal understanding and vernacular is comparable to his ability to operate a kayak. He can get out into the water, he can row safely back, but he'd be screwed if he capsized and went beneath the murky depths of Lake Titicaca.*

Man, that felt good to get off my chest.

I've been around the block. I've signed (dis)agreements, I've received advice on (dis)agreements, and I've created my own (dis)agreements. While I may not be a legal professional, I'm a guy who can see patterns and can identify the biggest stumbling blocks and considerations when discussing the ins and outs of collaborations.

When putting your (dis)agreement in place (whether verbal or formalized—though formal is better) you'll *need* to nail down the specifics. The more specific you can get, the better. Remember, ambiguity and non-clarity are not your friend.

Ahead, you'll find a breakdown of some of the key points that you *must* establish if you want your collaboration to have the longevity and prosperity that you are hoping for.

This list is by no means extensive. With each collaboration you may find your own niches or particulars that apply to whatever you're producing, but this serves to highlight the fundamental points that you should discuss and secure before you hear the starter's pistol.

(Dis)agreement consideration checklist

- 1. Deliverables
- 2. Timelines
- 3. Finances
- 4. Intellectual property (IP) rights
- 5. Contingency
- 6. The get-out clause

1. Deliverables

This is just a fancy name for the "thing you are producing", or the "product".

Are you strapping yourself in for a single novella? Is it a short story? Are you tying yourselves together for three novels? How about an entire universe, regardless of how many properties co-exist within?

This is the best place to start. Here, you are establishing what your end goal is, and making clear where you are both heading. Remember that time Armstrong and his comrades shot off in a rocket with no clear sense of direction and stumbled upon the moon?

No.

No, you don't.

Because it never happened.

Armstrong's team planned that operation to a T, knowing that they would land their rocket on the moon's cheesy surface, long before they'd even put a pencil to paper and started drawing diagrams.

That is now your task. Make clear what it is you are both going to work on. Make sure you're on the same page. Two people going in the same direction is productively faster than two people slowly drifting apart. Often you don't realize you've gone too far in opposite directions until it's almost too late to close the gap and recalibrate.

Start yourself off with the best chances of success. We may get a little deep into the weeds in the section ahead, but it'll definitely pay off in the long run.

Trust me.

2. Timelines

I'll repeat: set your expectations.

Like Baloo, without a timeline you'll just be drifting down a lazy river with no real urgency or purpose. Anyone can write a novel in twenty years—*anyone!*—but I'm going to assume you want things to move a little quicker than that.

Set the key dates for when you expect things to be complete. Be lenient and allow yourself some wiggle-room. Don't tie yourself in to unachievable deadlines. This has to work for both of you.

Key dates could include: first drafts, second drafts, editor handovers, pre-order upload dates, publication date, etc.

But they could also include the length of time certain IP rights will last against the product (which we'll go into in a bit).

Having a date, no matter how arbitrary it may seem, will put you on the best footing to kick off your collaboration. If you have some space in your calendar to complete a project in May, but your partner isn't free until September, then now is the perfect time to find out that information. Find ways to make it work, adjust and negotiate, but be sure you have *something* in place so you both know when you're working toward your goal.

3. Finances

There are two threads to this one.

Firstly, have you got any particular expectations with the division of royalties? Are you splitting the pot 50:50? Is it more 30:70? Make sure your rewards are fair and accurately represent your contributions. You both need to make sure you're happy here. You may not be thinking ahead to the finished product yet, but what happens if your work takes off and becomes an overnight success? You'll want to hash out rewards in advance to make sure you don't miss out on reaping the income generated from your hard work.

Secondly, is there going to be any substantial financial input into the project before it's finished? Is one of you going to front the money for covers? Is another going to pay for the editor? Is one person taking the brunt of *all* the expenses?

You can arrange the (dis)agreement however you want but be sure that it's fair. A number of (dis)agreements I've been tied into promise royalties will be sent to me *after* upfront costs are recouped. For example, if someone has fronted £500 for editing, cover, and launch marketing, my percentage of the royalties will not start rolling in until that £500 has been regenerated and placed back in the pocket of the original financier, which I see as more than fair.

4. Intellectual property (IP) rights

You are contributing in some way to a product together. It's worth taking the time to establish who will own what percentage of the property when all is said and done.

IP doesn't have to be tricky. It's one of those buzzwords that a lot of authors hate, but it's as simple as putting a claim on a product that is yours.

The IP distribution can vary depending on the project. If it's a straight up 50:50 novel, then of course you can both claim your 50%.

If you're writing in someone else's universe, it's likely that the creator of that universe will take ownership of that story, potentially returning full rights back to you within a number of years for your particular contribution (be sure to specify that number). It is their universe, after all, and they need to protect what's theirs.

If you're ghostwriting, then you'll likely have zero claim to the IP. But, then again, that's one of the things you sign into as a ghostwriter. You're in it for the art, not the glory.

Another strand of this sticky web is that you need to be specific over other strands of that property that, while they may not be in existence yet, could occur in the future.

For example, sure you're happy writing your future best-selling novel now, but have you thought of what might happen to the intellectual property after you publish? Does your (dis)agreement only count towards eBooks, or are you looking at paperbacks, too? You may not want to fund the audiobook right now, but what about if you do later down the line? Have you thought about comics? Film adaptations? Video game series?

Remember, anything not included in the (dis)agreement is literally anyone's game. That's where the messiness can come in, and it's in IP rights that I see most of the arguments take place.

All of these properties and adaptations may seem like a far-off dream now, but it's worth ensuring that you have your bases covered. Make this work for both of you and be explicit over any future possibility.

5. Contingency

This is the part that a lot of people miss, but it may be the most important to your continued legacy.

No one wants to think of what might happen if the worst should occur. Death is taboo in most areas of life, but it should be worth considering here. If left unspecified, the royalties that you've promised to pass on to your loved ones, might default into the hands of your surviving collaborative partner.

And what if they still hate you for spilling wine on their clean, white carpet. *Yes, I'm* still *looking at you, Katherine*!

Include a clause that mentions what should happen in the event of your death. If you are the sole administrator for the online dashboard in which your property is held, create a contingency plan. Make it easier to hand over properties and deal with the particulars following your demise.

Whatever you believe happens after death, I think we can all agree, you'll want the first few months of your passing to be as easy as possible on your loved ones. Don't skip this and give them yet another headache to fight.

6. The get-out clause

It may seem unnecessary, and it may be whittled down to a single line, but you're going to want to put in a way to terminate the (dis)agreement in case of emergency.

You'd never feel comfortable during the plane's take-off without having first sat through the laborious safety procedure. There's always a diamond hammer on the back of a bus. Every building has a fire alarm in case the worst should happen.

While I can't give you specific wording, I'd highly advise putting in a line that allows you to disperse the (dis)agreement under particular conditions and find a way to protect your IP. Hopefully, you'll never need it.

But what if you do?

Other considerations

I've avoided getting too granular here, as I want to give you the general overview without getting tied down in a thousand possible intricacies.

Your (dis)agreement will vary with each project. There is no template that'll fit your unique situation perfectly. In the appendices, I have provided an example of what a collaborative (dis)agreement *could* look like. I advise against copying and pasting this straight over to your collaborator. My specifics will be different to your specifics.

Still, other things you could include are clauses on:

- **Legal fees:** who covers the costs if you do get into a dispute?
- **Non-disclosure agreements:** do you need the silence of your collaborator in order to operate effectively?
- **Advertising and promotion:** Who's in charge of the

marketing side of your (dis)agreement? Is it equal for both of you?

- **Merchandise:** Are you including posters, t-shirts, and other merchandise in your (dis)agreement? How are the profits divvied? Are they unique to each platform in which the product is sold?
- **Particulars of production:** Which one of you decides the talent who will narrate your audiobook? Do you both get the final say on cover art?

And so on. The great thing about these (dis)agreements is you can add and edit as much or as little as you want. It's all really down to you.

A final note: check your work

Be sure that you're not signing a (dis)agreement blind. Sure, maybe you don't have experience with contracts and (dis)agreements, but you can at least show the terms and conditions to someone within your household, a close friend, or throw it out online to someone you trust.

- **Always get a second set of eyes on your (dis)agreement. A third, if necessary.** You may be tired when you first receive the (dis)agreement, you may be letting excitement get ahead of you. You'll undoubtedly miss things upon your first read-through. Get someone else to check for you and try to catch out anything that's missing.
- **Sleep on it.** It's in our sleep that our mind processes all of the information we've received that day. Even if you think everything is fine, allow yourself 24 hours to sleep and process it all. You may wake up and

remember something you wanted to include. You may realize that something is missing. No good collaborator should be rushing you to sign without due caution. You'll nearly always have the opportunity to digest it all first. (The only exception to this rule might be if you are working with a film studio or large production company who may have tight deadlines and need to get things moving. Even then, it's highly unlikely they'd rush a huge decision like that without giving you at least 24 hours' notice).

- **Get this right. This is your ticket to a successful collaboration.** You don't ride the twelve-loop without a secure harness and a team who provide the final safety checks. The ride is going to be fantastic, but not if you suddenly realized you've missed one clip, and it's only on the way down that the buckle flaps in front of your face...

5.3. COLLABORATION RED FLAGS

I've spent a lot of time going through the specifics of how to approach someone and reach out for collaborations, and even onto how you lay the foundations before you get stuck in to your project, but I haven't really touched on what to do if something doesn't quite *feel* right.

No matter whether it's you asking to collaborate, or someone else approaching you, there are some things that you should be on the lookout for.

Like with all great things, there are some sharks out there swimming in the water. These predatory fuckwits prey on the vulnerable and the innocent, looking for ways to boost their outputs without putting in any work themselves.

You want to collaborate, but you don't want to be taken advantage of. Before you sign on the dotted line, it's important that you're 100% confident that you're doing the right thing for you and your partner.

Below, I have listed a number of common "red flags" found in collaborations.

The following list is by no means extensive. If you come across any of these within your communications with your partner, take a moment to assess whether you think that particular collaboration is right for you.

They're reluctant to sort an (dis)agreement

While not an *immediate* red flag (I've already mentioned that *some* collaborators trust each other so much that they don't feel the need to create a written (dis)agreement), this is definitely a biggie in some cases.

Use your best judgement, here. If you don't know the collaborator from Adam, and you don't know much about their work style and processes, then you're in trouble. If your collaborator isn't willing to sign an (dis)agreement with you, it tells me one fact, plain and simple: they're trying to pull a fast one on you.

Depending on how "big" the author is, most will always have a template ready at hand. If not, they should be open to discussion about what the particulars may be. A true professional doesn't view the (dis)agreement as a negative document to introduce to their partner. I'd actually be nervous by any collaborator who doesn't mention making and signing a (dis)agreement somewhere along the way.

This is a great way to sift out those who are serious and those who are wasting your time.

No document, no collaboration. Simple.

No real commitment to timelines

This one again comes back to professionalism. I'm assuming that you're wanting to make a business of your author career. In which case, you *need* to know what timeframes you're working to.

Can you imagine strolling up to the marketing department in a corporate office and saying, "Hey, Helen. I need a campaign plan producing for that event we're throwing for underprivileged children."

"Sure, when do you need it by?"

"Oh, you know, whenever."

NO.

That's not how your business should work.

If you're entering into this project, you're already aware of your other commitments, you know what timeframes *you'd* like to work towards, you know how fast you can work. I'd expect a collaborator to know the same and to be able to negotiate timeframes that work for both parties involved.

If someone is unwilling to put down firm dates, or they're being woolly and evasive over the mention of confirming a schedule, again that shows me that you're not wholly serious about this project. You haven't thought it all through.

Either give them time to have a think or pull the plug.

Every second they spend not being able to manage their time, they're wasting yours.

You're giving way more than they are

There are some occasions where this may be okay. Again, use your best judgement.

Your gut instinct is your body's way of letting you know when something doesn't feel right. You know when something is wrong. If your gut is uncomfortable with the terms and conditions laid out in front of you, then the choice is wrong for you.

Don't get me wrong, sometimes nerves manifest in the body in the same way as excitement, but if you've promised a big-name author that you'll write the entire first draft of a book for a minimal fee and no royalties, then something isn't right.

All of this comes back to "2.3. Knowing your worth". Recognize that they couldn't do the work without you, and make sure you're getting what you're owed. The only person who ends up taking responsibility for a great or a terrible deal is you.

They're too pushy

"I need this back, ASAP."

"That's more than fair, just sign it."

"Given the amount of work *I'm* doing, you should be grateful."

Have you ever been bullied before? I have. It's awful. Bullies have a way of chipping away at your confidence and making you believe a false truth about yourself.

They'll convince you that they're better than you because of superficial reasons. They'll make you think your choices are your own, even though it was them who planted the seeds in your head. They'll *limit* your choices, and make you feel like your only option is to take the lesser of two evils.

Step back and return my lunch money, Richard! I'm twenty-nine!

If someone is trying too hard to get you to commit, the deal isn't worth the paper it's printed on. You think things will get easier after you sign? They've already given you a preview of what a working relationship with them will be like, so would you want to continue being treated that way?

There are a very limited number of reasons why someone can't give you the time to think. There are no excuses for someone being pushy or bullying you into making a decision.

There is a thin line here between eager and manipulative. The difference being that you can reason with an eager partner. Maybe someone is so excited that they just want to know that your project is going ahead. They're trembling with anticipation to have the chance to work with you and create something beautiful. That's a damn sight different to someone closing down options and giving you ultimatums. At least the excited ones are open to negotiation and talk.

It all comes down to your best judgement. Maybe you're not prepared to have someone constantly on the phone to you or messaging you every five minutes. In which case, even the eager beaver might be a bad fit for you. It's normally in this moment that people show their true colours.

Be careful. Protect yourself accordingly.

You feel insubordinate

The deal seems completely above board, and everything is fine. The only problem? You have no faith in yourself. You feel inferior to the person you're partnering with, and you're worried you're going to disappoint them and let them down.

To overcome this, you're going to need to be honest with yourself. Your partner has said "yes" for a reason, so you've done enough to convince them that you're a good fit together. If there are extreme worries, just be honest with your partner. Express your concerns and let them know what's bothering you.

I can safely say that I would give the upmost respect to any potential collaborator if they told me they were intimidated by me (not that I'm in any way intimidating, I might add…*okay!*). To make yourself vulnerable from the start and admit your worries gives me a chance to ease that pain and reassure you—my future collaborator.

Sure, maybe it might lead to a deeper discussion about how a collaboration may not be for you, but isn't it better to know that you're not committing to something that isn't right for months on end? Isn't it better to know that you don't have to hold the burden of your own fears and self-doubts and let them gnaw at you over time?

Coming at this from another angle, perhaps your lack of

confidence is coming from the fact that you've lied. You've BS'd your way through a cleverly worded email and you didn't think Mrs Big Shot would say yes. Well, she has, and now you're going to get caught out because you *lied*.

You lied! You reached this far through the book and you lied?!

I won't linger on the solution for this problem, I'll merely point you back a fair chunk of pages to "2.2. Honesty is the only policy", and hold your gaze with a judgmental eye as I say, "How the hell did you get this far in the book without learning to be honest?"

I'm not kidding, either. Every lie that you tell stores in your system and becomes poison. Those foundations we built? You've already placed them on quicksand. There are solutions but make them quick. The longer you leave it, the worse the fallout will be.

They try to introduce an invisible partner

No one likes a surprise threesome.

Okay, let me rephrase that. In Business, surprise threesomes are a bad idea.

If you're in the throes of negotiation and happily talking to someone about collaboration, you'd be right to raise your hackles when, from out of nowhere, your collaborator drops the line, "Oh, I'll have to run this past Sarah, first."

Who's Sarah?

Why is Sarah pulling any strings here?

Is Sarah a clever alias for you, Katherine?!

If this is the first time they've mentioned a third party in this collaboration, you'd be well within your right to question what's going on here. Does your collaborator already write with someone else? Are they already a partnership? Is this new guy the real head honcho behind your collaborator's business?

While collaborations of more than two people are perfectly acceptable (and sometimes encouraged), again we're falling into the territory of hidden information.

If someone is not upfront and *honest* about how they work when entering into a partnership, then that's a cause for caution. Find out more about this person; if their names are going to be appearing on a document you're signing, then you deserve to know all that you need to in order to make an informed decision. Are they wanting to give Sarah 20% overall royalties while you and your collaborator get 40% each? That's substantially less than you initially agreed.

Ask the question: who are they? However they respond to that question should give you some indication as to whether you have anything to worry about. Again, trust your gut. It's your body's way of letting you know what's right or wrong.

"Just trust me"

Why?

These three words are instant no-nos for me. "Just trust me," can be translated into any of the following:

- "You're stupid. I'm going to test that by seeing how much I can get away with, without you giving due caution."
- "I've got something to hide and no good explanation to cover my ass."
- "I don't have any solid answer, I'm just winging it. Join me on this reckless rollercoaster."

Don't get me wrong, you *do* need to trust your collaborator. You need to be able to rely on them and know that they're going to do the things they say they're going to do.

But, as much as we trust people in life, the truth is that people let us down.

Even my most trusted collaborations have (dis)agreements in place (now). People that I've known for years have put pen to paper and signed. It shouldn't be taken as an offence, it's just Business. An insurance policy. You can glide through life with rose-tinted glasses and believe that nothing will go wrong, but the truth is that people can let you down. Circumstances change. Life happens.

Anyone you're collaborating with should *expect* some kind of (dis)agreement to be put into place. If they're unwilling to zero down on the final details and they seem blasé about the whole damn thing, then hold them to account.

"Just trust me," is not okay. Now is the time to lock things down and put it in writing. I refer you to the previous section. Be explicit, be clear, sweat the small stuff.

Any *good* collaborator will be happy to comply.

Expert panel

Don't trust my word on any of the above? Then take a look at what some of my expert panel had to say when I asked them, "Have you ever had to say 'no' to a collaboration and, if so, why?"

 I knew our personalities wouldn't be a good fit.

— Jonathan Yanez

 Yes, because it wasn't a collaboration. It was a "I have this great idea, and why don't you handle it so we get a lot of money I just know it will be big."

— Michael Anderle

Yes. In three cases.

1. The author wasn't in a position to move the needle for me career-wise. It was in a genre I don't write in and the person wasn't established enough to make jumping genres worth it.

2. When it wasn't 50:50 but rather a paid gig.

3. This particular author is known to be a bit dramatic/precious.

— RAMY VANCE

 Only about 40 or 50 (hundreds if you include those who submitted to one of my anthologies). Either the quality of storytelling didn't meet my expectations, they were late, or they did something different from what they said they were going to do.

— CRAIG MARTELLE

 I have, simply because my gut told me to. It's so important to trust your gut, and to remember that, however good friends you might be with someone, you might not work well together.

— ANGELINE TREVENA

Notice the scale of criteria which span across everything from career-based decision-making, all the way down to gut reaction. If something doesn't *feel* right. It likely isn't.

5.4. SUMMARY

- **Laying the foundations.** Before you jump straight into writing, the most important thing you can do is ensure you've laid solid foundations. This is the point where most writers could fix all of their issues that may arise in the future. Be transparent, be explicit, don't hold anything back.
- **(Dis)Agreements.** (Dis)agreements are there for you when things turn sour. Make sure you have some kind of written agreement that you and your partner are equally happy with that covers all bases from now until way into the future. Anything not included in the (dis)agreement is anyone's game if things fall into dispute.
- **Collaboration checklist.** Be thorough when creating your agreement. While there are key points that each collaboration *must* include, additional options and extras are up to you to negotiate. Some of the core components to cover are: deliverables, timelines,

finances, intellectual property (IP) rights, contingencies, and the get-out clause.
- **Collaboration red flags.** If something doesn't feel right, it probably isn't. Trust your gut and pay heed to the examples in the chapter. Collaborations should be transparent from the start. If you think your collaborator is hiding something or is taking advantage of you in some way, call it out now before you sign on the dotted line and legally bind yourselves together.

COLLABORATION CASE STUDY: KATHRIN HUTSON

Kathrin Hutson is an international bestselling author of dark fantasy, sci-fi, and LGBTQ speculative fiction who has made a full-time living off her writing by publishing her own works, as well as bringing in an incredibly modest income through ghostwriting.

Kathrin's book, *Sleepwater Beat*, was a sci-fi finalist in the 2019 International Book Awards. She's continually juggling a number of different hats, able to consistently reach incredible word counts as she manages her ghostwriting among creating her own works and working as the fiction editor for the international literary journal, *Mud Season Review*.

I am continually in awe of Kathrin's work ethic, and when it comes to collaborating and speaking on topics such as ghost-writing, she was the first author I thought of reaching out to. Luckily, she was more than happy to answer any and all of the questions I had.

DAN: How did you first begin collaborating?

. . .

KATHRIN: I actually started working as a project manager and then later Chief Editor for Collaborative Writing Challenge (CWC). This was my first taste of collaborative work regarding anything in fiction (a full-length novel written in 9 months, one week at a time, one author per chapter). It was a huge process, and we published seven collaborated novels in various genres and a series of anthologies within a 3-year period. That might have been what got me hooked.

The same year I left CWC, I stumbled across a webinar for how to make six figures through ghostwriting fiction. Once I learned that this was a viable option for me (plus how possible it was and how much money I could potentially make doing nothing but living my dream of writing fiction full-time), I dove into the opportunity headfirst. That started my ghostwriting career, after a 12-month mentorship with someone who'd done the exact same thing, and one step led right into the next.

So, while I still write my own fiction and have big things planned for the future of my own work, I get to ghostwrite and collaborate full-time for a living!

DAN: What qualities do you look for in a collaborator?

KATHRIN: Reliability, dependability, and open communication are incredibly high up on the list. It's hard to get anything accomplished—or even planned—if those things don't exist.

This is closely followed by a meshing of creative compatibility. I'm sure there are people out there who I would not gel with creatively, and if I can pinpoint that from the start, it's a very good reason for me to say, "I don't think we're the right fit for this project." It's about working together and sliding all the pieces into place, so they fit well for all parties involved.

Despite the fact that my type of collaboration now is ghost-writing, the creative brainstorming and teamwork process is constant; it's never one person calling all the shots and the other person just dealing with it (and if anyone finds themselves in that situation, that's another good sign that the collaboration probably isn't a good fit).

DAN: HAVE YOU EVER SAID "NO" to a potential collaborator?

KATHRIN: Yes, I have. First of all, I know my limits very well when it comes to what genres I can write and in which styles. Romance as an entire genre is something I just can't do (nor do I enjoy it), and I'm okay with that. I tried writing Paranormal Romance once, and needless to say, I was not asked to continue that collaboration!

It's definitely important to know your own limits. And even when collaborating becomes a career, as it is for me, if you're not enjoying the projects you're working on from the very beginning, that's going to be very apparent in your work and the final product overall.

DAN: How has your collaboration affected your individual work? (Speed, quality, efficiency, education, etc.)

KATHRIN: All of the above! Collaborating as a career and with an income I can rely on through various contracts has been one of the biggest motivators for me to kick my butt into gear and really start flying with my writing, specifically when it comes to speed and efficiency.

I remember when I started out writing my own fiction with the aim of turning it into a full-time career that writing 1,000 words a day seemed like a *lot*—though still completely manageable. Now, I'm averaging 13,000 words a day (writing five days a week), and that doesn't include the work I do on my own books (which is about 2,000 words a day on top of the ghostwriting).

I can also say that I have learned *so* much about different styles of writing, different tropes in a variety of genres, and a whole new world of "what readers want" through collaborating on and ghostwriting so many books for clients. Now, it's gotten to the point where I'm opening up a different "branch", if you will, of my own fiction that incorporates what I've learned for collaborating into my own special brand of dark fiction. I'm so excited to see what happens with these new series and to test how well I can pull this off on my own and under my own name.

Note: I will also say that I currently have a mentor for this new series. That's a different form of collaboration. I'm taking two different styles and blending them with my own as a "best of all worlds" à la carte experiment. The minute I start thinking I know everything and don't have anything left to learn is the minute I seriously need to stop and take a complete inventory of what I'm doing wrong. I hope that day never comes!

DAN: What is one (or more) common myth that you hear about collaboration that just isn't true?

KATHRIN:

- Collaborating is harder than doing it yourself
- Your creative freedom is stifled when collaborating

- You lose your own voice and style completely when collaborating

DAN: How have you tackled any situations where the collaboration was in jeopardy or didn't match your expectations?

KATHRIN: This is where open communication is *so* key! Whenever I hit potholes in the collaborative road (and while those are few and far between now, I'd be lying if I said I haven't come across my fair share of them starting out), I go immediately for honesty and opening up a space on my end for my collaborators and I to discuss what went wrong and how we can improve.

99% of the time, that's all it takes. Is it incredibly humbling? Absolutely. Has it led to even stronger and more beneficial relationships and projects for all parties involved? Yes, yes, and yes.

I've also found that when collaborators aren't willing to enter that space and speak openly with *me* about what's going on and how we can all improve to alleviate the issues, those collaborations rarely continue after that.

More than anything, for me, it's about being willing to do whatever it takes (within reason and without grinding myself to the ground, because who wants that when they've already got their dream job?) to ensure that what I'm working on is, first and foremost, a good story, with quality writing and characters that readers can't get enough of.

I've had to step up my game more than once to make that happen. While it was hard at times, and once or twice made me feel like I was losing my mind, it's been more beneficial for me in the long run than I ever could have imagined.

· · ·

DAN: How important are contracts and agreements to a collaborative project?

KATHRIN: Contracts and agreements for timelines, payment (if applicable), and scope of work are *so* important. These are a safety net for all parties involved, and they help keep everyone on track while also knowing what's possible and when. It's a fantastic tool for gauging how a first-time collaboration is going to work out.

DAN: What, in your opinion, are the main benefits of collaboration?

KATHRIN: I mean, for me, benefit number one is that collaboration literally pays my bills and supports my family. That's a pretty big one for sure.

Beyond that, I'm well aware of the fact that I don't know everything about everything, that I can't come up with "all the great ideas" by myself, and that I have so much more to learn from others than I could ever learn on my own. Plus, the challenge of blending collaboration with my own process for writing fiction (and keeping deadlines all while writing my own books) is where I've found I really thrive. It's easy to let things slip through the cracks when we are the only person we have to be accountable to. But when you're a part of a collaboration that has so many different moving parts, there's that extra pressure there to do my part to the best of my ability so everyone else can do the same.

And yes, I thrive under pressure, too.

. . .

DAN: Are there any softwares or systems that are fundamental to your collaboration?

KATHRIN: Nope. I'm just over here doing my thing, and I'm happy to say that, when it comes to the collaborations, I work within a professional capacity, the only thing I'm responsible for is crafting the story. That's also one of my favourite parts.

DAN: What one piece of advice would you give to someone looking to get involved in their first collaborative project?

KATHRIN: Try it! Understand that it won't be easy, and there will definitely be moments of needing to put aside what you think you know about how *you* do things (and maybe a bit of swallowing one's pride in the process). But if you really open yourself up to the possibilities and look at collaboration as an opportunity for everyone to grow, learn, and benefit in ways not quite available to you on your own, you may just find that it's your cup of tea. Or you may not, and in that case, at least you have your answer.

PART VI

GETTING STUCK IN

6. GETTING STUCK IN

Congratulations, adventurer—you've made it!

You've cleared every hurdle that stands in your way to collaborative paradise, and now you're here, staring up at the oak front doors of your new collaboration, hands clutching the shoulder straps of your backpack...

...as you try not to hurl.

I jest. This is the fun bit! You've taken every possible step to ensure that your collaboration is exactly what you wanted, you've got someone invested in the idea, you've signed on the dotted line, and now it's ready to get into the creative stuff.

I'm not going to give you a step-by-step guide on *how* to collaborate. That bit is up to you. What I *am* going to do over the next few sections is introduce you to a particular set of tools that will make your journey as collaborators all the easier to navigate.

The 21st century has done wonders for collaboration. Jump back even twenty years and people were faffing with fax machines. Jump back another fifty, and it was all about that snail mail, baby. Imagine trying to collaborate in the 1800s, before the telephone was invented. It would be nearly impossible!

Technology has really given us some of the most amazing tools to collaborate. Dozens of individuals can jump into an online document and edit at the same time, changes and document history can be tracked, we've got tools at our disposal for research, finding answers to the impossible questions, and collecting images and video at the touch of a button. There are video conferencing platforms, tablets that act as paper, reading devices made of plastic.

I could go on...

There is *literally* no better time to collaborate than right now. Don't believe me? I'll prove it to you.

I've divided the chapter into four categories:

- **Ideation and story:** All you will need to keep track of your world, characters, and plots.
- **Marketing and planning:** Want to keep track of roles and responsibilities, links, resources, and have a single place to make sure you're on track and ready to launch? It's all here.
- **Publication:** Who's in control, and what are the best ways to publish together?
- **Financial tracking:** Because what's Business without knowing the numbers?

I WILL BE transparent and say that I have no affiliation or links with any of these services mentioned ahead, I am just a happy customer and have found great benefits in my own experience. There are a thousand more tools out there, you may want to find the ones that work for you. Or, you can just shortcut and steal mine.

6.1. IDEATION AND STORY

Collaborating on a single project together can get messy. Soon enough, you and your partner will have emptied the Lego box, mixed everything in with the Play-Doh crate, and now neither of you can find Buzz Lightyear's missing arm, or the cartoonified meat steak appendage which makes the T-rex roar.

You're going to want a system, a way to keep everything in order and track what you're doing. You may need online file-sharing hosts like DropBox, Google Drive, or OneDrive. But I'm not here to tell you which are the best services to organize your folders, I'm here to tell you the best ways to track the 80-headed hydra before he runs off into the distance and chews up the village.

With story and ideation, things can get particularly messy. It's hard to marry two people's processes, especially if you're working on separate files. It's probably worth discussing your processes and how to make things work for you guys. Don't feel like you have to follow one person's method because they think it's best. Your opinion counts, too.

Over the next few pages, I've outlined some of the most fundamental, and tried and tested methods to getting your collaboration underway. Become familiar with "the cloud" because it's going to be your friend. And, yes, I mean the digital cloud, not those wispy things blocking my perfectly good view of the sun.

Who am I kidding? I'm in England. What the hell is sunlight?

～

Google Docs
docs.google.com

THERE ARE a number of software packages that do what Google Docs does, but none quite so efficiently as this.

For those of you more accustomed to Microsoft Word, Google Docs is pretty much just the online version. Sure, its functionality is a little more modest, but it's an online word processor that lets you type, format, and view your written documents online.

Why am I recommending this over Microsoft Word? Simple...

- **Instant backups.** Any changes you make are uploaded and saved every few seconds. There's no need to worry about losing any progress you have made if your computer craps out. All of those times you've forgotten to plug your laptop into the mains and realized only as the screen grows black that you haven't saved your file? Forget about it. Docs saves your files automatically, and it's all there again when you log in.
- **Multiple users in one file.** Thanks to the magic of the internet, multiple users can access a file at once.

You can easily view who else is "in" your document with the handy icons in the top right of the screen, *and* any changes your collaborator is making on the document, you can instantly see. This can be a little strange to get used to, but it has its uses. You can both minute your meetings as you talk, and jot down ideas in case you forget anything in the future.

- **Tracked history.** While you may not need this one that often, Google Docs keeps a running tab of any significant changes as the document is edited. That means that you can check up on your collaborator and find out when they were last in the doc and ensure they're holding up their end of the bargain. Sneaky, eh?

- **Comments, replies, notifications.** Also a fundamental function of Word, you can add comments to certain parts of the document and reply instantly to your collaborator. You can also tag each other and send live updates to your email inboxes (if you wish), so that you both get alerts when things need tending to.

Google Docs is nothing short of the very minimum you need to make your life as collaborators easier. I've used Docs for countless ideation meetings, as well as planning stories, and even managing the first and second drafts of a project. With Google Docs, there's nothing left hidden. All that you need is out in the open and stored in one place, and it's great for getting the words down and having a single document that both of you can reference when you need it.

Pro tip: Two writers, one manuscript

For those of you who want to work fast, have one person start writing the first draft and, a few hours later, let the second collaborator dive into edits immediately behind them. You could literally be the broomstick to your collaborator's ice curling efforts as you both go, increasing the pace of your edited project.

Scrivener
literatureandlatte.com/scrivener

SCRIVENER MIGHT NOT BE everyone's favourite tool for collaborators, but it has its uses.

Scrivener is a great program for keeping thoughts organized and planning your worlds. The main selling point of Scrivener is its binder system and its ability to reorganize and track large sections of your document more intelligently than other programs.

You know those moments when you need to move an entire chapter, or you'd like to see a summarized overview of the entire narrative? Yeah. You can do that pretty easily, here.

Scrivener also has functionality to connect with services like DropBox so that you can easily share the latest files with your collaborator. While you can't both dive into a project at once, if one of you is taking the lead on planning, and another on first-drafting, then this is a great program to get down those words and track it all. With its host of research folders, and character and setting templates, it's incredibly easy to keep track of all the intricacies of your novel, too.

Scrivener also supports a host of export tools to get your files ready to upload to Kindle and other dashboards. Personally, I'd rather use a program like Vellum for this, but Scrivener gives you the option.

For a one-time fee of around £50, Scrivener can serve you well. You may have to invest a little time into learning what it can offer you, but it's worth it in my opinion. Scrivener is open on my computer pretty much all the time.

(It's also what I wrote this entire book in).

Story bibles

WHILE NOT NECESSARILY A PROGRAM IN itself, it's worth exploring ways to create story bibles.

Story bibles are both God and the Devil—I mean that figuratively and literally. If you're like me, you often get carried away in a story and forget a lot of specifics of the earlier tale whenever you need to recall information.

"What was the protagonist's mum's name again?"

"She grew up in Illinois, but what was the colour of her favourite teddy bear when she was five-years-old?"

"Are his eyes blue or green? *Blue or green!*"

We've all been there. Building a story bible is a colossal pain in the ass. It's the equivalent of stepping on Lego, stubbing your toe, and being told you misspelled prooofread all in one go (yes, that was deliberate).

Story bibles *can* be a lot of work to maintain but depending on how big your project is going to be, they're well worth it. The more time you invest in creating and *maintaining* a story bible, the more time you save from having to look things up later or switching character names by accident.

Creating a story bible doesn't *have* to be hard work, though. If both of you are chipping away at it and doing your part, then a story bible is just another part of the process. With my own work, I don't often dive out of a chapter that I'm working in just to update a folder and let someone know they have a cousin called Larry. What I *will* do is wait until I've finished my writing session, and then upload any new information into the correct boxes. I don't worry about formatting or making it nice, I literally copy chunks of text, "He had a scar running from his lower eyelid to his upper lip, and eyes a pale yellow, like the shade of day-old bruises", and dump them into the folder raw.

However *you* choose to manage your story worlds and track what you're doing is up to you. Luckily, there are a few services out there that are great at this kind of thing and can be incredibly useful for keeping those ducks in their row.

One additional note, you'll also want to avoid spending hours in world-building and story bibling. Sometimes it's better just to crack on with writing your story, and world-building can become a time suck rather than a benefit. Use your time wisely.

～

StoryShop
storyshop.io
(Free "Lite" version, approx. £79/year for "Pro")

STORYSHOP IS a program built by writers for writers. With a few years under its belt now, StoryShop acts as a one-stop-shop for collaborations. Build your world piece by piece, level by level, and save it all in the cloud. With StoryShop, you can create characters and take advantage of their "social media-like" interface to connect your characters, keep track of their minutiae, and link them back to your text.

One great thing about StoryShop is that when you're done, you can simply switch to the "Writer" mode. Here you can link back to all of your notes and start crafting your story all on the same program. Similarly to Google Docs, StoryShop's paid version allows two of you to enter the world at once and edit at the same time.

Why didn't I recommend this to start with? Well, if you're a newbie to collaboration, you're likely going to want to reduce your overheads. StoryShop has a lot to offer and is great if you take advantage of it all, but I'd argue that it's a luxury rather than a necessity.

~

WorldAnvil
worldanvil.com/author
(Free "Freeman" version, £41/year for "Journeyman")

IF ALL YOU'RE interested in is the world-building element of a program, then WorldAnvil may be useful for you.

A robust, diverse program, WorldAnvil is great for niche genres, like science-fiction and fantasy. You can build world timelines, create articles for your characters, and take advantage of prompts to build your characters. You can build maps and family histories all within its easy-to-use interface. You can also publish all of your behind-the-scenes work for your readers to see, if you wanted to provide them with additional content around their favourite books.

WorldAnvil provides a deep rabbit-hole you can get lost inside. If you're going to be building rich and varied world-scapes, this is great for you. However, heed my previous advice. Don't spend *all* your time on world-building when you could be writing.

~

Scrivener
literatureandlatte.com/scrivener
(Approx. £50, one-time download fee)

WORTH AN ADDITIONAL MENTION, Scrivener offers a more robust system than Google Docs and is also an offline service. With Scrivener's binder system, you can create folders for your characters, settings, and props all within easy reach of your story. With its backup systems and sharing capacities, this may be your better solution for on-the-go writing, and it saves you some money, too.

NO MATTER what you use for story bibling, just remember, that it's your world, you do it your way. Whatever works best for you is the best solution. It's easy to get lost in the void of finding the perfect program, but when all is said and done, getting the words on the paper always takes priority.

6.2. MARKETING AND PLANNING

Whether you're independently published, or sitting pretty with one of the "Big Five" publishing houses, you're going to want to find a useful way to streamline your tasks and distribute things between you and your collaborator so that as few of the twenty-seven balls you're juggling hit the floor.

I've bundled marketing and planning together because, in my experience, they're the two which require the most checkboxes. Planning will, no doubt, start from the very beginning, and may be as simple as:

- Write first draft
- Source cover artist
- Make list of book promoters
- Editing complete
- Publish

However you choose to organize yourself is entirely up to you. It's not my job to dictate how you plan and market your books, but instead to gently lower your waxed paper boat into the lake and give it a gentle nudge into the wind.

(Watch out for Pennywise...)

Marketing will contain a bunch of its own checkboxes and it's very useful to note down everything you can think of in terms of giving your book the greatest success possible when it launches. When you're knee-deep into your first true mind-mapping session, it's worth utilizing some powerful tools which are available to you in order to ensure that you have everything organized and ready to progress forward.

Creating a road map is also the best way to ensure that you remain on task and accountable through the whole process. Can things change along the way? Well, yes. Sometimes Lil Donnie needs the restroom. Sometimes traffic jams force you onto a B-road. As long as you have an end destination, and a specific set of points along the way, you're bound to get to where you're trying to go.

A word of caution before you proceed...

If you're like my past self from... twenty-minutes ago, then you'll likely spend an incredibly unnecessary amount of time trying to find the *perfect* planning companion. With an App Store on all devices that sports hundreds upon thousands of apps all designed to do the same or similar things, with each declaring they're better than the other, it's easy for your mind to get over-whelmed with decision fatigue.

I can't count the hours I've spent downloading new apps, copying over all my tasks, only to realize that I preferred the app from three tests ago. Still... What about this new one that has fancy branding and says it can bring me Jack Daniels whenever I'm feeling like I want to smash a hammer through my screen?

Don't get stuck in the mire. One thing I've learned over the years is that it's easy to get distracted and place all of your hopes on an app to do the work for you. No matter what you download, your app is only as great as your dedication is to that app. If it's not working for you, move on. Try something else. Maybe you are a pen and paper guy. Maybe you have an eidetic memory and can store that information in that grey gooey bit between your ears.

Great. What are you wasting time browsing apps for?

The programs I recommend in the following sections are ones that I've personally used and still benefit from today. They're the cumulation of at least three weeks' worth of head pounding and brow creasing. I have preferences over some more than others, but everyone has their own kinks and loves. As with all recommendations so far, find what works best for you, and if you find others that have amped up your productivity and streamlined your planning, get in touch and let me know for future editions of this book.

NOTE: Mobile Apps

It's worth mentioning that all of the recommended programs do have brother and sister mobile apps. Some are better than others, and it's up to you to decide whether you want to give your pocket-sized best friend more reasons to buzz and disturb you throughout the day.

(You can see where my feelings lie on the subject...)

Asana
asana.com

 "Asante sana squash banana, wewe nugu mimi hapana."

— Rafiki, *The Lion King*

WHILE ASANA HAS LITERALLY nothing to do with Disney's *The Lion King*, I always end up singing that song when I sign in.

Asana is a project management tool designed and fronted by one of the original mind-brains behind Facebook, Dustin Moskovitz. While it isn't as addictive or news-nourishing as Facebook, you can already tell that a lot of time and energy has been invested to make Asana a robust system for collaboration, organization, and planning.

Whether you're a fan of to-do lists, or Kanban boards, Asana offers a lot of versatility within its program. Even the free version can work great for getting you on the road and getting things underway. The key thing with Asana is that it's customizable for the way that you work, and that is where its strengths lie.

Collaboration

Asana makes it incredibly easy to add one or more people into a project. Between you, you can see a live and up-to-date version of where you are with your tasks, and you can leave each other messages and notes to follow things up when required.

Checkboxes

If you're like me and get pleasure from satisfying spine shudders when you check off your to-dos, Asana can grant you that feeling. Not only can you click and tick away the tasks you've completed, you occasionally get little animations celebrating your wins. Multi-coloured birds, magical narwhals, and fireworks are just a few of the animations I've personally witnessed.

Who doesn't love an app that doubles as your personal cheerleader?

Kanban boards

If you're more of a visual person who likes the idea of tracking projects with mini tiles on larger boards, you can also set your project up in this way. While other programs build their entire interface around Kanban boards (Trello, for example, which we'll come to), Asana has managed to integrate the option rather elegantly. Within each "board" you can also then dissect tasks further into checklists if you need to.

Deadlines and notifications

Asana allows you to assign projects and tasks to particular collaborators, while also setting deadlines and providing notifications to ensure these are hit.

There's a nice little section on the top left called "My Tasks", which allows you to see only the tasks which have been set for *you*. This is a great way to filter out anything that might seem overwhelming when looking at a project as a whole and allowing you to focus on the next most important thing.

File sharing

You can drop images, Word files, PDFs and more, straight into any of the tasks for easy access and sharing. Asana is a great way to store research or to get feedback on book covers and keep an online log of what you've done and how you've managed your project.

Project boards

If you're managing multiple projects, then Asana lets you easily create entirely new boards for each one. This is a handy feature for those who are managing multiple worlds, or even those running a publishing company and managing multiple authors or projects.

You can also set access controls to each project so that only those who need to see what's going on can. Lock out the nosy ones and include the key ones. Oh, the power...

Pro tip: Once you've completed a project, you can duplicate the project board and you've instantly got a whole checklist in place and ready for your new project. Save yourself time from listing everything all over again, by just doubling it up and tweaking your process on your next project.

Templates

If you're struggling to work out where to start on Asana, they offer a range of templates designed to help with a multitude of situations. Just click one of the available templates and dive straight in! Most of the work is done for you.

Timelines

If you're upgrading to the Premium version, and you're a fan of Gantt charts (bleurgh, corporate speak...) then Asana can handle this for you with a clean, flexible interface to keep an up-to-date overview on *all* parts of your collaboration.

This is especially handy if you've got a lot of collaborators dipping their hands into your cookie jar.

Todoist

todoist.com

KEEP IT SIMPLE. Keep it elegant.

Todoist is just one of a thousand to-do list programs that make it easy to track individual tasks. Why am I recommending Todoist over the others? The answer is simple.

Because I *could* have spoken about *any* of them.

If you don't want to faff around with boards and project lists, then there are a whole host of simple to-do apps you can download and take advantage of. I like Todoist because it prioritizes your next most important tasks. Find out what you're up to this week with a simple glance. It also allows you to colour-code your projects (I can hear the hardcore planners out there already drooling), and choose whether your task is associated with home, work, or any number of categories you choose.

One tip from me if you choose to go down this route: don't get bogged down in trying to combine all of your home, work, and personal tasks together. Keep your software dedicated to one facet of your life. Otherwise you're mixing your colours with your whites with your DVD player.

Somehow, you're going to end up blowing up your washing machine.

Simple

To do apps like Todoist are simple. There's nothing in the way of learning curves. You simply have to create a task and check it off when you're done. Apps like this, I find, are best managed on mobile devices, but again it's up to you how you play.

Categories

While categories are not always necessary, they're handy to have. This allows flexibility for working on multiple projects, or even to look at the stages of certain projects: red equals planning, orange equals production, yellow equals marketing, and green equals launch.

Clean overview

The benefit of a lot of these apps is you can view your most important tasks at a glance. Some offer "Today", "Tomorrow", and "Next Week" views, while others organize theirs slightly differently.

Notifications

An optional extra, most of these apps have the capacity to sort reminders and notifications to keep you on track. In my experience, it's always worth the extra few seconds to plan your timelines than leave things ambiguous and undefined.

Daily habits

With Todoist (among others) you can set up recurring tasks and habits. If you want to plan your day down to the minute, you can include things like: "Workout", "Meditation", "Check email", and any other regular activity that you would include in your ideal workday.

∿

TRELLO

trello.com

I'm going to go ahead and guess that, for many of you, in Section 6.2.1 Asana, you learned a brand-new word: Kanban.

Well, Trello is the king of Kanban boards.

Kanban boards are a fantastic way to get a visual overview of where you're at with a project. There's enough versatility that you can manage your own columns, and the tiles can shift easily between the columns depending on where you're at with a project.

You can organize a Kanban board from the operational level (specifics of "is this task complete"), or you can look for a macro level (are we on track to publish book X, Y, and Z).

Like Asana and Todoist, Trello has its own free version which is great to give the software a trial run, and it's fairly customizable in terms of adding backdrop images to projects and the entire interface.

Trello is fantastic if you're looking to streamline the amount of bulk you put into your planning. There's room to go in deep and heavy, of course, but it's up to you where you'd like to take it. Its simple interface is clean and easy to view from a top-level.

Collaboration

Trello is another program that makes great use of being able to invite individuals into your project and share content. It provides to-the-second updates and allows you to manage the permissions of individuals, too.

Kanban boards

This is where Trello excels. Its entire interface has been designed and moulded around the Kanban board premise, and therefore is smooth and, I'm going to say it, flawless.

If Kanban boards are where your heart and head lay, then look no further.

Checkboxes

If you prefer looking at top-level checkboxes, you'll be left disappointed. While you can add lists of checkbox tasks *within* boards on Trello, this functionality doesn't exist elsewhere.

Still, it's great having your checklists organized and easily accessible within the boards themselves.

Deadlines and notifications

Trello makes deadline setting and notifications simple. In much the same way as the other two programs, scheduling reminders and keeping yourself on track is the main bedrock of this program.

File sharing

File sharing is, once again, made easy by simply clicking and dragging files for you and your collaborator to share. Images show up as previews and can help decorate those boards if you're a visually inclined planner.

Project boards

Trello boasts multiple levels of Kanban boards. Your top-level shows boards of all of your projects, then you can go into each one and set up your sub-boards accordingly.

Similarly to Asana, this is a great way to keep a top-level overview of all that you're working on, especially if you're managing multiple projects or looking after other authors.

Templates

Not dissimilar to Asana, Trello provides new users with a number of templates that are easy to browse through and select the one that'll work best for your project. Not sure where to start? Maybe in a place where all the heavy lifting is already done for you.

6.3. PUBLICATION

For me, being in control of my own publication is the reason that I remain, to this day, an independent author.

That's not a sleight against anyone searching for traditional publication, but it will mean that this section is likely more relevant for those who are fully in control of their publication process.

The moment you click "Publish" something magic happens. Your work, that you and your collaborator have spent weeks, months, years on, goes off into the intervoid, where it will be processed by word-goblins and placed in the public sphere of wordestry.

A mixture of emotions bubbles inside you. You're not sure if those tears are excitement at what's to come, or fear of the critics. Your palms are sweaty. Knees week, arms are heavy...

Maybe that's enough Eminem.

Still, if this isn't your first publishing rodeo, then you're usually used to celebrating alone. Revelling in the achievement that you've solely been responsible for. But now you've collaborated, and you *finally* have someone who has been there across every level of the process with you. I love publishing with other people, because the celebrations are just that much sweeter.

Don't get me wrong, I've tried to emphasize to ex-girlfriends about the trials and tribulations and hoops I had to jump to just to get to the finish line, but there's a disconnect. You know as well as I do that no one understands the pain of publishing your words, other than your fellow writers.

And now you get to bask in that glory—together!

Grab a beer, pour some champagne, jump on Skype or Zoom and high five the screens (don't break the camera). Your hard work has finally gone public, and that's amazing.

Unfortunately, this chapter isn't on how to celebrate reaching the finish line of creating the book (notice I didn't say the finish line of the project, you've still got to sell, sell, sell!). This chapter is about how you can handle the publication process. As usual, there are a few options, here.

"I volunteer as tribute"

ONE OF THE simplest routes to go down is to have *one* person manage the publication process entirely. We've all heard the phrase, "Too many cooks spoil the broth." Well, let me be the first to say that there's truth there, even if you're writers and not chefs.

You've spent a hecka-while perfecting your book, the last thing you need is to cock up the publication. For first-time publishers, there are a bunch of niggly stages that can easily get missed or screwed up if they don't have your undivided attention. Not only are you ensuring that you upload the correct book file, but you've got to pay attention to the cover art, the key words, the descriptions, the book pricing, the categories, the series name, the author names, the publisher names, and so much more.

Sure, some of these steps hold more weight than others, but if you have more than one person trying to get all of your ducks in a row, then you're more than likely to be spending more time trying to keep the mallards out of the casserole than you would be if you tackled this solo.

Too many mixed metaphors?

Let me simplify. If two collaborators try to set everything up at once, you may find that you *believe* your partner has done something, when they haven't. Not maliciously, I hope. Maybe they were distracted. Perhaps a bumblebee flew in the window, or their latest copy of Maxim came through the letterbox. Whatever it is, I highly recommend that one person take the lead, here. It'll serve you both well in the long run.

Have one person set up the publishing process in their name. Allow them to be the sole person responsible for setting up the publication.

Pro tip: Share the moment

Of course, you both want to share in the delight of hitting publish, and while only one of you has taken the lead, here, this is still possible.

Jump on a video call and share the moment that one of you presses the "Publish" button. You can still revel in the finality of your product going live, while reducing the chances to mess up the launch.

Trust me, it happens.

∽

"We're all in this together"

THIS CAN BE a bit of a grey area, but it's my preferred method of approaching this, *primarily when publishing several collaborations with a single author partner under a publishing imprint.*

I mentioned at the start of this book the story studio that I manage alongside my four other directors, Hawk & Cleaver. In order to manage all of our publications, we own a shared dashboard in which Hawk & Cleaver books are published and stored so we can look at how books are selling at a glance.

The aforementioned grey area comes from the T&Cs of certain services. A handful of publishing companies do state that you should only have one publishing dashboard per author name (I'm a naughty boy, and I currently have three). While there doesn't seem to be a *strict* policy on this, it's worth mentioning just in case you encounter problems with this approach and end up shouting at this book on the bus and find yourself incarcerated for a night.

Shared dashboards make things a thousand times easier to organize... in *some* situations.

If you're looking at a one-off collaboration, then I'd recommend picking one of you to take the lead.

If you're looking to publish a number of titles under your own publishing imprint, and one or more other authors are essential to the operation, then creating a shared dashboard in the name of that imprint makes a lot of sense.

Rather than sharing a thousand accounts with a thousand different authors, you can simply store all of your collaborations on one dashboard and, if necessary, you've got a set of credentials that you can hand over to your partners to login and check their books for themselves.

Pro tip: Only share login credentials with those you *trust*. If you're looking to run a publishing imprint under *your* name, you'll want to keep the dashboards as close to you as possible. If you're running a publishing imprint *with* other authors, then only give the credentials to those for whom it is necessary to operate the business.

∾

Anthologies and multi-author box sets

BundleRabbit
bundlerabbit.com/home/collaborate

DEPENDING ON YOUR PUBLISHING GOALS, there are alternatives out there to make handling collaboration a lot easier or everyone involved. However, BundleRabbit is a great service for those who are looking to publish multi-author anthologies and box sets.

While the books may not be published on mainstream services like Amazon or Kobo, BundleRabbit offers a great way to publish your book alongside other authors and gives everyone involved access to view the books and keep an eye on the analytics.

The main disadvantage, of course, is that you'll be selling books away from the main stores where readers find their books. However, this is a great way to sell your books wholesale and increase your profit margins, while providing a little something extra for your newsletter list which cross-pollinates with similar authors.

This may be a little more niche, and something that you maybe hadn't considered, but anthologies and multi-author box sets are a great way to grow your reader list while networking with other authors in your genre. BundleRabbit isn't the *only* way to do this, but it definitely makes sense in a lot of ways.

Plus, the service only takes 10% of the overall royalties, *and* takes care of handling all of the financial side of things.

More on that in the next section.

Pro tip: More than anthologies

BundleRabbit isn't *only* for anthologies and multi-author box sets. You can publish your collaborative novels there, too.

6.4. FINANCIAL TRACKING

The elephant in the room.

I'm unable to speak for other countries, but as a UK-born, bulldog-loving, beer drinking, consumer of fish 'n' chips, I've always been raised to believe that discussing finances is akin to whipping out your member at the Sunday family roast and rubbing it in the roast potatoes.

Take from that what you will.

The truth in collaboration is that you *will* need to discuss finances. If you're in this game to make money and potentially turn endless keyboard-smashing into a productive and worthwhile career, then you're going to have to talk brass-tax.

Hopefully you've already been open and honest about your situation at this point. If you're maxing out credit cards and desperately hoping that the repo men don't come knocking on your door, then you best have let your collaborator know that you can't chip in £300 for a book cover. With finances, as with every aspect of collaboration, transparency is key. You should never feel forced into a situation in which you have to front money that you're uncomfortable letting go.

And that's before we've even spoken recompense, which is where this section will focus.

I'm again assuming that you've discussed financial reward in your agreement that you set up as collaborators. If you have been promised 50% of all royalties earned, then the equations are simple. The one thing you'll have to work out is how best to process and distribute finances when they come in.

Are you both going to share the login for a particular service? Have you spoken about getting a shared bank account? Would you rather one person handles the finances and give you what you're owed while the other manages their share of marketing or stays out of it completely?

We come back to one of the fundamental values of collaboration: *trust*.

No matter which way you roll the dice, you're handling real-life, hard-earned, substantial amounts cash. That comes with its own risks. The green-eyed monster can strike at any time. If you can't trust your collaborator at this point, head straight on back to Chapter 1 and start the process again.

If you *can* trust your collaborator, then bully for you! Still, there are many ways in which you can slide open the window of transparency and ensure that you're both in a position to manage your own share of the finances.

The world of independent publishing has opened up so much over the last decade that there are an increasing number of services in which you can view finances and even distribute royalties easily to authors you've worked with. Of course, in the beginning, this might require some heavy lifting from one person or another, but over time you may find yourself in a position to hire a financier for one day a week or month to handle it all for you.

Ah, that's the dream.

If you're ever in a position in which you want to check the

royalty statements and view the balance sheet, you should always be able to ask. Even if management of finances does not directly sit in your lap, be cautious of anyone unwilling to show you numbers. As much as we like to believe it's the magic of words that binds us, most of the lifeblood of ensuring we remain successful as authors is hidden in the numbers.

So, how do we keep everyone in the loop and distribute accordingly?

~

Abacus
publishdrive.com/abacus.html

ONE OF THE biggest reservations for people looking to collaborate is the worry of handling and distributing finances to co-authors.

I get it. Can you imagine having to painstakingly sit and examine bank accounts, royalty statements, manage people's account details, and dealing with queries and questions about products sold and the various levels of percentages taken between the wholesale price and your final amount?

Fortunately, services like Publish Drive's *Abacus* have come along to take a lot of the pain out of the process.

It's pretty simple to use, too. All you need to do is:

1. Create a login
2. Import your books
3. Setup any particulars in terms of royalty splits
4. Export your data

The great thing about this is that both collaborators view an up-to-date, accurate version of the royalty statement in case of any queries. You don't need to bug each other to see how a product is performing, you can simply log in and sort it.

When the month-end comes (or whatever date you choose to get paid), you can then just ship the money over.

While this isn't a free service, the cost is reasonable. All Abacus asks for is $2.99 per book title, per month (with the first title permanently free). So, if you're planning on making at least $3 on a book per month (which, I hope your expectations are high enough to find that achievable), you've already got your fee covered.

∾

Book Report
getbookreport.com

BOOK REPORT IS a handy extension that can be added to Google Chrome and Mozilla Firefox browsers. It provides a comprehensive and user-friendly way to analyse and view your book sales and royalties for any books published through Amazon's "Kindle Direct Publishing" (KDP).

To use, simply load up your KDP dashboard, and click on the Book Report extension button in the top right of your browser. Book Report will then open up a tab through which you can view the latest sales, figures, and page reads. You can see which books are performing the best and find out where your main income streams are coming from.

While not so much a collaborative platform, if you and your partner have decided to publish through a shared KDP dashboard, then you can both log in and view statistics. If only one of you has access, then you can download reports for your collaborator to read and look through each day, week, or month.

BundleRabbit

bundlerabbit.com/home/collaborate

THE ONLY SERVICE in this book to get multiple entries, I bring your attention once again to BundleRabbit.

I'm not going to spend a lot of time here, considering I covered a lot of this service's functions in the previous section, however it's worth an extra note thanks to the way BundleRabbit handles its financial services.

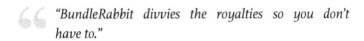

> *"BundleRabbit divvies the royalties so you don't have to."*

— BUNDLERABBIT WEBSITE

It says it clear on its front page. If you're looking to publish collaboratively, you don't have to worry about processing all of the finances, the service does this for you.

Whether you're publishing with a single author, managing box sets, or launching an anthology, software like BundleRabbit can remove all of the additional labour once your book has been published.

Though, remember that services like this won't see your book published on platforms like Amazon, Kobo, Apple Books, or Google Books. Be intentional about how you're choosing to publish and what you'd like to get out of each book before choosing your publishing and financial management services.

6.5. SUMMARY

There are a thousand ways to collaborate, but here is a roundup of a number of useful tools that can help make your collaboration run smoothly.

Ideation and story.

- **Google Docs:** An online, cloud-based word processing software that is capable of handling multiple users at a time. Simple to use and a must-have for various elements of collaboration.
- **Scrivener:** Great for offline work you share with your partner, though doesn't benefit from cloud-based storage.
- **Story Bibles:** You'll want to have a central database to store all of your story information, so you don't lose anything. There are some options out there:
- **StoryShop:** A comprehensive online platform to plan stories, created by authors, for authors. Can be costly.

- **WorldAnvil:** Specifically designed to build worlds. Great for fantasy and science-fiction authors.
- **Scrivener:** Simple and safe, Scrivener's binder function is great for classic worldbuilding within a document.

Marketing and planning

- **Asana:** The most diverse of the project management programs with list view and Kanban functionality built straight into the code.
- **Todoist:** To do lists are simple and great for getting things done. Find one that works on your app store that allows sharing with your collaboration partner.
- **Trello:** Great to get an overview of projects and utilize Trello's Kanban functionality. A different way to plan each stage of the process.

Publication

- **"I volunteer as tribute."** One person takes the bulk of the responsibility when it comes to parsing the finalized project through the publishing process. Removes possibility for errors and mistakes.
- **"We're all in this together."** Collaborators share dashboards so each party has access to the files and the publication process. Great for transparency, preferred for longer-serving partnerships.
- **Anthologies and multi-author box sets.** Work alongside other authors, with one person taking responsibility for uploading and editing the

collection to publish. Services like BundleRabbit are great for simplifying this process.

Financial tracking

- Abacus: Handles the accounting and sales side of your published project so both parties can view real-time financial reports, while one collaborator acts as admin. Divvies out royalties and streamlines the process for you both.
- Book Report: Great if you're sharing a KDP dashboard to see the statistics and royalty reports from your collaborative projects. Easier to digest than the native KDP reporting page.
- BundleRabbit: Simple to divvy royalties across multi-author box sets, anthologies, as well as collaborative books which you choose not to publish on the main self-publishing platforms.

COLLABORATION CASE STUDY: LE BARBANT

L E Barbant is an author of science-fiction and fantasy. His collaborative partnership with author CM Raymond has birthed almost two dozen novels in which both of their names are printed on the cover. Together they oversee *The Age of Magic* and *The Age of Madness*—two fictional timelines that exist within Michael Anderle's *Kurtherian Gambit* universe.

Both LE and CM manage a number of authors writing within the universes as well as juggling their own collaborative series alongside this. LE and CM were my first mentors when it came to writing within someone else's universe and acted as coaches to get me off on the right footing. They have been on all sides of collaboration and I couldn't be more thankful that LE found the time to answer my questions and share his viewpoints on collaborating.

DAN: How did you first begin collaborating?

LE: I kicked around a book on my own for six months or so and completed two chapters I wasn't happy with. So, you could say solo authoring isn't really my strong suit. Then a friend of mine (CM Raymond) mentioned that he was looking for someone to write a series with and we were off to the races.

Every book I've ever published has been with CM. In addition to our own collaboration, we got connected to Michael Anderle and the LMBPN world through our podcast and that opened the door to dozens of other collaborations.

We wrote the *Age of Magic* series with him within his Kurtherian Gambit world, and other authors published books within our *Age of Magic* and *Age of Madness* (something like 8 additional authors... I've honestly found it hard to keep track).

DAN: What qualities do you look for in a collaborator?

LE: The creative arts can be a vision-centric place, and it can be really difficult to open your mind once you've set it on a particular path. This makes collaboration almost impossible. So, I look for folks who are open to the idea that stories aren't set in stone—that there's not one right way to tell it—and are willing to brainstorm and compromise and... you know... collaborate.

But the other end of that is equally important. You need someone who is going to be committed to the story, which requires advocating for a character or an arc or a plot point. The only thing worse than an iron-fisted partner is a laissez faire one. This can be extremely difficult to know before the work starts.

DAN: HAVE YOU EVER SAID "NO" to a potential collaborator?

. . .

LE: I don't think I ever said no to someone outright, but there are a handful of folks I have written with where, after we finished the project, we more or less agreed not to work together again. Some of that was clashing visions or inequitable weight carrying, but most of the time it had to do with the headache factor.

Making a book is hard work. Making one with someone else is doubly hard. If you don't feel good with the finished product, then the headache isn't worth it. And I know that I cause headaches for the folks who work with me! But I hope that what I offer as a partner is worth that frustration, that it's frustration for the sake of something better.

A lot of this is impossible to know before you actually start. You can read someone's solo work and love it, only to find that they don't have the same kind of energy around your joint project. Or maybe they just had a killer editor last time that you should have worked with instead.

DAN: How has your collaboration affected your individual work?

LE: This is a bit of a mixed bag. On the positive side, I've learned so much about the craft and business of this weird industry. Having someone read drafts alongside you—offering suggestions and ideas and encouragement—is the best education you could receive. You can get some of that from a good developmental editor or from reader feedback, but it's not quite the same as when it's from someone who has real stock in the project.

There's a million and one lessons I've learned from co-authors that I'm taking with me into my solo work. But... I'm also taking with me a lot of bad habits. Chris and I figured out pretty quickly where our individual strengths lie. Which means we can lean on each other effectively. But that means I've spent years polishing the parts of my writing that I'm already good at or at least inclined to enjoy, while letting Chris carry the load on stuff I suck at. It's important, especially if you're planning on collaborating long term, not to let your other skills atrophy.

DAN: What is a common myth that you hear about collaboration that just isn't true?

LE: That it saves time. It does not, at least not in my experience. At least not in terms of publishing faster. I've been able to work on more projects at one time because I've had collaborators, but I don't think a book has ever been published faster because several people divided the workload. At least not if all parties are equally committed to quality.

DAN: How have you tackled any situations where the collaboration was in jeopardy or didn't match your expectations?

LE: There's nothing worse than trashing a project that you've invested significant time or energy or hope into, but the sunk cost fallacy is a real danger when it comes to shaky collaborations.

If you can have an honest conversation with your partner, then sometimes you can fix the problem. Oftentimes you can't. There have been a couple of cases where I powered through the problem just to get it done. And every time I was dissatisfied with the final product. There have been a very few cases where the project had to be junked, and I honestly lay awake at night thinking about them. So, it's kind of a lose-lose if things go south.

One thing that I've had middling success with is bringing on another collaborator. Sometimes a third party can solve the problem that two people working together can't.

DAN: How important are contracts and agreements to a collaborative project?

LE: I think, when it comes to the rights side of things, then a contract is necessary. But when it comes down to the "who is going to do what" side of things, finding a partner you can trust is essential. And if you've found that kind of partner, mapping out the jobs/hours/responsibilities isn't as important.

DAN: What, in your opinion, are the main benefits of collaboration?

LE: There are a ton of benefits. Better quality, the ability to get more of your ideas into the world, the division of labour. But honestly, the best part is that it makes the whole thing way more enjoyable. When you've got the right partner, this job can be an absolute blast. I'd pick that over being a lonely writer any day.

DAN: What one piece of advice would you give to someone looking to get involved in their first collaborative project?

· · ·

LE: Do as much work as you can on the front end; tight outlining, test prose chapters, clear character outlines. Make sure you are both on the same page in terms of vision and tone. And then... be willing to hold that stuff loosely if and when better ideas emerge. Because better ideas will emerge.

PART VII

WHEN COLLABORATIONS GO WRONG

7. WHEN COLLABORATIONS GO WRONG

Sigh...

Those who know me know that I'm something of an upbeat guy. I like to look on the brighter side of life and will often choose optimism over pessimism.

"Is the glass half-empty, or half-full?" they'll say.

"Is it full of sunshine? How about rainbows and unicorns? Someone fetch me my happy blankie and fix me a mug of hot chocca because today's going to be fantastic!" I'd reply, eliciting a show of creased brows and tutting tongues at the witches waiting for me to boil into mulch in their cauldron.

I mean, I jest, but I *was* reticent to include this chapter.

The reality of collaborations is that, sometimes things don't work out. Sometimes you find that your partner expects too much from you and you can't deliver and keep pace. Sometimes the book tanks on release and all you're left with is resentment and bitterness as you throw punches and try to assign blame. In some cases, failed collaborations can lead to a breakdown of real-life friendships.

This is why I included the sections in Chapter 2 of this book. The entire foundation of the collaboration is the most important part of the whole process. Without being honest, setting expectations, knowing your reasons for collaborating, and all of that other good stuff, you're already setting yourself up for failure.

I get it, sometimes life gets in the way. Perhaps you've placed all of your chips on the table, hoping that this collaboration would be your rocket ship to stardom, and you've just discovered that your collaborator can no longer remain involved due to personal issues and commitments—that's going to suck.

The greatest piece of advice that I can give in any degrading collaborative situation is this: you can only remain in control of your own reactions.

I've been fairly careful throughout this entire book to tread around the pit of psychology. I'm in no means claiming to be an expert in understanding the human psyche, but I do know this one thing that has helped me with my own collaborative situations. You may find that three months down the line something has become an obstacle in your collaboration and your partner has resorted to obscenities and blame for your involvement in the project.

Be calm. Breathe. Emotions are always going to be heightened when two humans are cuddled closely in the cupboard together. Things are going to slip out of your control, the only thing you *can* control is how *you* react to it.

There's an ancient saying, cast down through generation after generation. A simple phrase that holds the answer to all of your problems:

"Hakuna Matata."

Yes, I'm serious. When a collaboration *does* go wrong, it's worth taking a second to put everything into perspective. If *you've* done all that you can to ensure that you held up your end of the bargain, you've followed all the steps in Chapters 2–5, then you have nothing to be sorry for.

Sometimes the breakdown of a collaboration can be the best thing for you.

Let's be honest, with collaborations, as it is with dating, people can lie to you. For the first few months they can show you their best self and put on a mask like "Yes, I adore horror movies, I watch them every week", and "Oh, my God. I hate mess, too. I hoover, like, three times a day", and, possibly, "I'm a gym freak, too. I can't go a day without getting my sweat on, hee-haw". Then, three months later they're slouched on your sofa, surrounded by sweet wrappers, chocolate stains around their mouth and watching *Frozen 2* for the fifth time that day because they have to try and drown out the nightmares of watching that guy chop off his own leg in *Saw*.

People lie. People fake. I don't think it's deliberate, I choose to believe that people really *want* to believe the best in themselves, so they create the persona of the people they want to become; but time erodes all things and the truth cannot hide. Soon their mask slips.

It's going to happen. You can't escape it. All you can do is try to find the positives in the negativity.

If you've been smart and put some kind of get-out clause in your (dis)agreement and ensured that you can protect any IP produced between the pair of you, then I bet you're now glad you've got your lifebuoy wrapped snuggly around you. Now, you can walk away with your head held high. You tried, you failed. It happens.

But, ask yourself: if your partner has just shown their true colours, would you even want to be associated with that guy or gal anyway?

Dust yourself off, princess. It's time to get back in the game.

I'm not going to go all corporate and produce a flowchart of how this all works, but if your collaboration has devolved into nothingness and you've found yourself alone on a wooden raft, stranded out in the ocean as the naked sun beats its rays down on your skin, then paddle your ass back to shore and return yourself to the beginning of the book. Every negative experience in life is an obstacle and challenge to learn from. So when you gave your best friend the benefit of the doubt and they ended up disappointing you, now you know what to look out for next time.

You've hardened yourself to adversity and you, my friend, are so much stronger because of it.

Maybe collaboration isn't for you.

The worst-case scenario here is that you've taken the time to read this book, got on-track with a collaborator, and suddenly discovered that you don't enjoy the process. You hate other children playing with your toys and the product you've created doesn't represent you.

That's okay, too. You tried. With your get-out clause you can negotiate a smooth out, and potentially find a way to keep relations positive with your former collaborator. Not every single breakdown needs to end in anger and violence.

I circle back to "2.2 Honesty is the only policy". It's as true then as it is now. Don't drag something out for the sake of it. Would you want your partner to spend months believing you're in love with them, when secretly you yearn to be single and live a life of your own choosing?

Dragging things out only increases the pain for both of you. If you're experiencing doubts from the get-go, then be honest. Have the painful conversation then. The longer you leave it, the more painful it'll be for both of you, and the greater risk of a fallout.

Bonus article:

If you'd like to read a first-person experience of a true collaboration gone wrong, you'll find an essay that was kindly donated to me from an (anonymous) author friend entitled "Writing with the enemy" in the appendices at the back of this book.

PART VIII

8. EXPERT PANEL: FINAL WORDS FROM THE PROS

While this book has been splattered with useful content sent over by my incredibly generous band of expert authors and collaborators, as we close in on the end of this book, I thought this a perfect time to ask the single most powerful question that can help set you forward into your prospective collaborations.

The following replies were given in response to the question, "What is your number one piece of advice for first-time collaborators?" While you'll note that some of these have been included earlier in the book, here you can view them all as one to remind you of some of the key lessons we've shared over the last several hundred pages.

 What are you bringing to the collaboration? Know your why and make sure that the person you are collaborating will take it as seriously as you do. If you have a volatile life, consider putting off the collaboration if you can't make your due dates.

— MICHAEL ANDERLE

> *Trust your gut. Nothing is more important. While you should always be open to changing your mind about someone, trust your instincts.*

— ANGELINE TREVENA

> *Get to know the other person well first. Make sure you're on the same page and get along well.*

— H.B. LYNE

> *Don't be precious about your words.*

— RAMY VANCE

> *Underpromise and overdeliver which means you better know your limitations as an author.*

— CRAIG MARTELLE

> *Do as much work as you can on the front end; tight outlining, test prose chapters, clear character outlines. Make sure you are both on the same page in terms of vision and tone. And then...be willing to hold that stuff loosely if and when better ideas emerge. Because better ideas will emerge.*

— LE BARBANT

> *Make sure your writing partner is strong where you aren't.*

— (JONATHAN YANEZ)

Try it! Understand that it won't be easy, and there will definitely be moments of needing to put aside what you think you know about how YOU do things (and maybe a bit of swallowing one's pride in the process). But if you really open yourself up to the possibilities and look at collaboration as an opportunity for everyone to grow, learn, and benefit in ways not quite available to you on your own, you may just find that it's your cup of tea. Or you may not, and in that case, at least you have your answer.

— Kathrin Hutson

 Be open and don't get in your own way.

— Luke Kondor

 You can come up with a bunch of really cool ideas together. But if you get into the process and things start falling apart, none of that's going to matter. Starting with a short story or doing a few short stories or a novella is a really good way to test the waters and see how you're going to work with somebody else.

I would also add that you should try to work with someone who has similar experience to you. If you've published a few books, and you are working with a first-time author who's never even worked with an editor before, that could have some challenges with it.

— Zach Bohannon

GO FORTH, YOUNG COLLABORATOR

We made it. Give yourself a pat on the back and go hug your new collaborator. You've both entwined yourself in something truly special.

They say that misery loves company, but the same is true of excitement, passion, and wonder. Collaboration is something that, for me, heightens the emotions of the book publishing process. I love having someone alongside me on the ride, to bounce ideas off of, to test me and challenge me, and make me a better writer.

Collaborations give us a chance to become greater than the sum of our parts. The watch on your wrist is a collection of a thousand pieces of intricacy working together at once to tell you something as simple as the time, your phone is nothing but hundreds of micro-chips and electrical impulses, the foods you eat are a combination of micro-ingredients which enrich and nourish your body and life.

Collaborations have the capacity to create something unique from two partners who share a common goal. Sure, sometimes they can go wrong, and we know enough now to dust ourselves off and move on, but in a lot of examples collaborations *do* work, and they're fun, they create something that lasts beyond the initial collaboration.

Ask any actor who has spent the last six months of their lives on set or stage with their cast members. Ask any employee who has sat next to the same colleague for three years. In working intimately alongside someone, your relationship transcends that of a normal friendship and becomes a permanent fixture in your life. When a collaboration is over, you'll forever have the memories of the times you shared together, or you may even decide to continue the work indefinitely.

I've collaborated with dozens of people over the last half decade, and I have no intention of stopping. Collaborations are addictive, and a certain excitement I feel in the very marrow of my bones comes with looking to where and who you can collaborate with next. We've spoken a lot about the specifics of collaborations when it comes to the art of writing, but I haven't even mentioned the cover artists, the editors, the digital managers, the accountants, the virtual assistants, or anyone else who could be deemed a collaborator if you're working with them on a regular basis.

The beauty of the human condition is that we have the right to choose what we do, we have the right to share what we want to share, and we have the ability to brighten people's day and help others in the same way that they can help us when times get tough.

Maybe you've come to the end of this book and realized that collaborations just aren't for you, that's completely fine. You do you—and I don't mean that in the passive-aggressive way that my ex used to shout at me when I told her I would put the bins out when I was good and ready—I mean that, sincerely. Knowing yourself and how you work best is something that comes from time and experience, and we can't all love the same things. Knowing you don't want to collaborate is just one extra thing you can rule out to perfect *your* process along your author journey.

But, let's be honest for a moment, I bet you're damn tempted to give a collaboration a try.

Ahead of you now is an open road filled with a thousand opportunities. Go forth, young collaborators, and forge your own path. Use this book as a reference guide to set you on the straight and narrow. Leave a review, share the word with your peers, collaborate with me by helping me spread the message of this book.

But, most of all, I wish you all luck, joy, and prosperity on your collaborative journeys.

Peace out, for now.
Daniel Willcocks

THANKS (AND BONUS CONTENT)

Thank you for reading *Collaboration for Authors*. I hope you found it useful and that it has helped you take steps towards your first collaboration.

Please consider leaving a review for this book and sharing with any writer friends who may also benefit from its contents. Your support is appreciated.

As a bonus for making it all the way to the end of the book, I have provided some additional content that will help you along your collaboration journey. These include:

- A link to download your **FREE Collaborative Partnership Agreement template** you could use with your own collaborations (or visit www.danielwillcocks.com/writers)
- Profiles of each author in the "expert panel" for this book
- **The original blog post** I wrote way back in 2016 which outlines the specifics of the process Luke Kondor and I followed when "Co-writing Two Books" at once, also known as my first official collaboration

- **"Writing with the enemy"**—a first-hand view (by an anonymous author) on a collaboration gone wrong.

EXPERT PANEL MEMBERS

Once again, I'd like to say a massive thank you to every single author listed below, who took the time out of their busy schedules to contribute to this book. Without you, this book would be one man's equivalent of shouting into an echo chamber, but with your valuable insights and generous sharing of your experiences, you've made this book all the richer for both reader and writer.

MICHAEL ANDERLE IS the author of the successful Kurtherian Gambit books and Universe. Michael boasts collaboration efforts with over thirty authors in some capacity—both as major partners and very minor partners. He is the founder of 20Book-to50k® and LMBPN Publishing.

LE BARBANT IS A FULL-TIME PITTSBURGHER, part-time professor trying to cut it as a science fiction and fantasy author. A fan of classics—new and old—Lee tries to write books that take an honest look at the world and then say screw it, let's find a better one. Because who wouldn't want to live in a world where super-heroes were real? You can find his collaborations on his Amazon page.

Zᴀᴄʜ Bᴏʜᴀɴɴᴏɴ ᴡʀɪᴛᴇs post-apocalyptic science fiction, horror, and fantasy. He is the author of the best-selling zombie series, *Empty Bodies*, as well as the best-selling post-apocalyptic horror series, *Final Awakening*. He's the co-owner of Molten Universe Media

Nɪᴄᴋ Cᴏʟᴇ ɪs a former soldier and working actor living in Southern California. When he is not auditioning for commercials, going out for sitcoms or being shot, kicked, stabbed or beaten by the students of various film schools for their projects, he can be found writing books. Nick's book *The Old Man and the Wasteland* was an Amazon best-seller and #1 in Science Fiction. In 2016 Nick's book *CTRL ALT Revolt* won the Dragon Award for Best Apocalyptic novel.

Kᴀᴛʜʀɪɴ Hᴜᴛsᴏɴ ɪs an international best-selling author who has been writing Dark Fantasy, Sci-Fi, and LGBTQ Speculative Fiction since 2000. With her wildly messed-up heroes, excruciating circumstances, impossible decisions, and Happily Never Afters, she's a firm believer in piling on the intense action, showing a little character skin, and never skimping on violent means to bloody ends. Kathrin is an active member of SFWA and HWA and lives in Vermont with her husband, daughter, and two dogs. Find out more at www.kathrinhutsonfiction.com

. . .

LUKE KONDOR STARTED MAKING stuff on his computer in his early teens and never looked back... and now he has really sore eyes. Check out Luke's books, films, and games over at www.lukekondor.com

H.B. LYNE LIVES in Yorkshire with her husband, two children and cat. When not juggling family commitments, she writes dark urban fantasy novels, purging her imagination of its demons. Inspired by the King of Horror himself, Holly aspires to be at least half as prolific and successful and promises to limit herself to only one tome of The Stand-like proportions in her career. Other interests and idols include Joss Whedon and Robert Kirkman, and she will often be spotted wearing Firefly or The Walking Dead apparel.

CRAIG MARTELLE HAS OVER 100 books published, over 4 million words written, over 5,000 Amazon reviews, and over 25,000 Goodreads reviews. Stop by www.craigmartelle.com and join his newsletter for five free short stories and one free audiobook.

J. Thorn is a Top 100 Most Popular Author in Horror, Science Fiction, Action & Adventure and Fantasy (Amazon Author Rank). He has published 2 million words and has sold more than 185,000 books worldwide. He is an official member of the Science Fiction and Fantasy Writers of America, the Horror Writers Association, and the Great Lakes Association of Horror Writer, as well as the co-founder of Molten Universe Media. Find out more about J. at www.theauthorlife.com

. . .

ANGELINE TREVENA WAS BORN and bred in a rural corner of Devon, but now lives among the breweries and canals of central England with her husband, their two sons, and a rather neurotic cat. She is a dystopian urban fantasy and post-apocalyptic author, a podcaster, and events manager. Find out more at www.angelinetrevena.co.uk

RAMY VANCE IS a Canadian who lives in Edinburgh with his wife, a four-year-old demon and imaginary dog. He enjoys a beautiful city, whisky (Scottish spelling, not his) and long walks. He writes kickass Urban Fantasy thrillers set in the GoneGod World (and elsewhere). Currently his greatest aspirations are writing more stories and finally get that real dog so he can have an excuse to go on even longer walks.

JONATHAN YANEZ IS the internationally published winner of the Jack London Award, as well as the Director of Content at Archimedes Publishing. Find out more at www.instagram.com/author_jonathan_yanez

ACKNOWLEDGMENTS

Collaboration for Authors wasn't a book I had planned on writing this year, but a few people were instrumental in making it happen and pushing me towards what you now hold in your hands.

I'd like to first of all say a huge thanks to Sacha Black, whose encouragement and endless patience against the volley of messages and questions and calls thrown her way has been admirable, to say the least. I was already teetering on the edge, and you threw the tennis ball at the back of my head, so thank you.

I'd like to thank every single person I've collaborated with in book, podcast, and script form to get to this point in my career, including: Luke Kondor, J. Thorn, Michael Anderle, John L. Monk, and Jon Freeman. A thanks to all the incredible authors who contributed to this book, and the multitude of authors who are out there sharing their knowledge with the world. I've always been a huge consumer of podcasts and non-fiction books, and each one has contributed invaluable lessons which have in some form wormed their way into this book.

A special thank you to my advanced readers, as well as

Elaine Bingham for combing through this book and putting it into some kind of shape that is presentable.

Thanks to my mama and papa who taught me how to play nicely with others.

I'm sure I'm missing out people in these thanks, if I am, then reach out, scold me, and I'll tweak these pages in the second edition.

GAWD!

ABOUT THE AUTHOR

Daniel Willcocks is an international bestselling author and podcaster of dark fiction. He is one fifth of digital story studio, Hawk & Cleaver, co-producer of the multi-millions downloaded iTunes-busting fiction podcast, 'The Other Stories,' as well as the host of the 'Great Writers Share' podcast, in which he breaks down the strategies, tricks, and productivity habits of some of the best writers in the game today.

Residing in the UK, Dan's work explores the catastrophic and the strange. His stories span the genres of horror, post-apocalyptic, and sci-fi, and his work has seen him collaborating with some of the biggest names in the independent publishing community.

Visit www.danielwillcocks.com to find out more.

facebook.com/willcocksauthor
twitter.com/willcocksauthor
instagram.com/willcocksauthor

LISTEN TO THE PODCAST

It's no secret that writing can be lonely work, but does it really have to be?

Join Daniel Willcocks every Friday as he hijacks an hour or so of time from some of the kindest and hardest working writers around today, so he can pick apart the tips, tricks, and strategies that make them successful.

AVAILABLE ON ALL GOOD PODCAST APPS

APPENDIX

HOW I'M CO-WRITING TWO NOVELS WITH @LUKEOFKONDOR

This was the original blog post I posted on www.steemit.com way back in 2016. It was my way to lay out a picture of what Luke and I were doing, as well as spread the message of our method and hold us accountable by announcing our project in public.

This project went on to spawn three novels: *They Rot* and *They Ruin*, both books in a single series that's still ongoing today, as well as *Lazarus: Enter the Deadspace*, a standalone that clocked in at a little over 100,000 words.

There is little I would change about this collaboration. It gave us all the lessons we needed to learn to work together and create stories that we were, and remain, proud of. This blog post is verbatim, as I didn't want to alter any of its original messaging when sharing with you. Take from this what you will, it's not a perfect methodology, but it worked for us.

WELCOME TO PROJECT DAN. An idea spawned from the minds

of two indie authors, and egotistically claimed by one. With one simple objective:

Two writers. Two books. Half the time.

Now, I know there are some people that have been keeping up and have heard me harping on about Project Lazarus, and some stuff to do with the awesome Luke Kondor. But I've not exactly outlined what's going on.

Well, here's the LD.

A few months ago, myself and fellow Hawk-head Luke Kondor (author of *The Hipster Who...* series), joined creative hands and decided to try co-writing. Neither of us have co-written before. Neither of us had a clue where to start. But we threw caution to the wind and dived in.

After a few weeks of idea tossing and planning, we created a timeline, and a formula for how this would work. Knowing that we each have our own strengths, and our own quirks, we wanted to maximize productivity, without stifling creativity.

And thus, our process was born. We (and by "we", I mean Luke) titled this **"Project Dan"**.

Project Dan works as such:

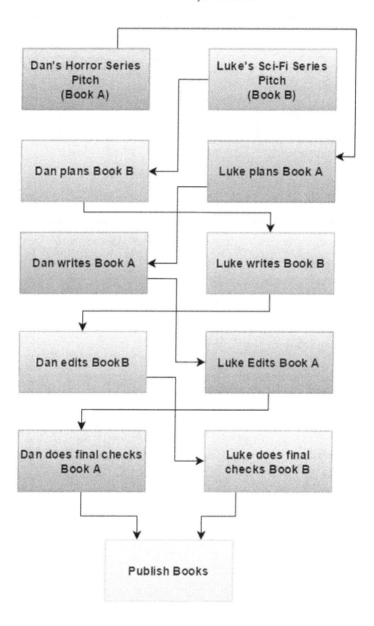

Seems simple on paper, doesn't it?

Now co-writing was something that I never planned to do. But there are a few distinct advantages of co-writing that I've already found.

1. There's someone besides you, going through the same things you are.

Now this is important. One of the hardest parts about writing is that constant battle with loneliness. You're shut up in your workspace with no one there to tell you that all is going well. "Good job, Danny boy. That's a best-seller right there."

Having a co-writer means that, although we're leading separate projects, we're running the same deadlines, we're hitting similar walls. We have someone that we can talk to.

2. All the ideas!

So, the above flow chart might seem complicated, but it has already thrown a tonne of ideas into the mix. By swapping story ideas and allowing the other person to plan the books we want to write, we get fresh eyes, fresh creative juices, and just a whole new perspective that broadens your horizon of what the story could be.

So far, I see no negatives here.

3. Super productivity.

Our main motivation for Project Dan is this. We both want to write books. We both want to produce great content. We have similar ways of working. By working together to produce two books at once, we're doubling our chances of publishing books quicker, sacrificing nothing in the way of quality, which also means that we're more likely to please our readers.

And that's the ultimate goal here: providing great quality stories to entertain our audience.

If there's one thing that I've learned over the last couple of years of writing, it is that everything comes down to trial and error. What works for some people may not work for others. The writing world is an ever-shifting organism that has no time for your shit.

So far this has been working for us. We are both currently writing the first drafts of our books, tentatively titled:

- Book A: "Lazarus"
- Book B: "They Rot"

These will be the first of their series, with some great twists and turns already planned. We hope you'll join us on this journey and keep up-to-date with us over at www.hawkand-cleaver.com

WRITING WITH THE ENEMY

WRITTEN BY ANONYMOUS

In fiction writing, and in non-fiction too, viewpoint is important. What follows is told from my point of view. It is *my* side of the story. My collaborator would doubtless recount the same events in a completely different way. I say this so you're aware that you're only getting half the story.

An old friend discovered I was a writer and contacted me on social media. This has happened a few times over the years. Usually I exchange a handful of messages with someone and we discover that the only thing we have in common is that we went to the same school a couple of decades ago. But this was someone I had collaborated with on a few things—writing and performing some comedy and publishing a few humorous bits. We'd always talked about grander projects—a sitcom or maybe a film—but then we'd gone our separate ways and hadn't been in contact for a few years. But the fact that we hadn't spoken to each other for ages didn't seem to matter in this case. We still sparked off each other and more or less picked up where we had left off. Or so it seemed.

Since I was now writing and self-publishing, we decided to collaborate on a novella. As you do. I thought it would be something fun to do alongside the other fiction and non-fiction projects I was working on.

My collaborator lived in another part of the country, so we decided we'd collaborate remotely.

My preferred method of communication when I'm working with someone else is e-mail. It's less intrusive than always-on messaging and makes keeping track of communications and attachments easier. He didn't want to use e-mail—he wasn't on top of his e-mail inbox to the extent I was. He wanted me to sign up for a commercial document sharing platform that he used for work. I read the terms and conditions and they basically said that he, as the account holder, was responsible for my use of the platform; that any documents created there were his, and that he had the right to lock me out at any point. As a writer, that rang alarm bells for me. I don't give up control of my work that easily—and by "control" I mean intellectual property rights and the kind of control that a control-freak like me needs to have on a daily basis. I said "no" to using the platform and we ended up collaborating via a messaging app.

It may look as though I was ignoring all sorts of warning signs here—but this was not a big budget thing in terms of cash or my time. I was still regarding it as a fun side-project.

Next we needed to agree what sort of project we were going to work on. We exchanged lists of favourite movies to see what titles we had in common. My list has all sorts of genre stuff on it, including action-adventure and horror. His list had a lot of arthouse and foreign language movies. We agreed that where our tastes overlapped best was on a movie like *The Maltese Falcon*, so we agreed we'd write a novella something like that.

Again, there are obvious warning signs here, but I didn't see them at the time. They only became apparent to me later. While I like some arthouse movies and mainstream literature, as a *writer* that is not what I do. I have no illusions about my writing

—I write *genre* fiction. I do properly structured plots, quirky characters, and humour. Macabre humour. And there are some arthouse movies that definitely leave me cold—Ingmar Bergman movies, for example. He had two or three Bergman movies on his list.

Here's the problem with *The Maltese Falcon* that I didn't spot. You can view it in two different ways. To me it is one of the finest examples of the private detective genre, both as a novel and as a movie. But to others it is arthouse *film noir*. You're a writer, you can see how this set-up is going to play out...

Like most writers, I have several notebooks full of ideas—physical notebooks and files on my computer. I had an idea that I thought would work for our private eye novella, so I put it out there and we agreed to work on it together.

In days gone by, "working together" for us meant we sat in a room and bounced ideas around. I would make some notes and then I'd go away and turn that into a finished skit or story. That worked pretty well and I (mistakenly) expected that we'd work the same way again now. We bounced ideas around for "Son of Maltese Falcon" and then I went off and wrote a rough first draft. I write quickly and had the draft done in a couple of days. This was not received well. I don't mean that he didn't like what I'd written—he didn't like that I had written it. On my own. Without him. But he didn't tell me that—not until much, much later.

In the years that we'd been apart, he had decided that he was now a writer too. He'd written a short story. He sent it to me. It was very short, impressionistic, and plotless. I didn't hate it, but it wasn't the sort of thing I write. As tactfully as I could, I said that I liked the story but thought the ending was a bit rushed. He said that this was done deliberately for effect and that my opinion must be wrong because the story had been accepted for publication in a magazine. The kind that doesn't pay contributors anything.

I shrugged this off, but I shouldn't have. I've been writing since I was eleven years old. The hard drive on my PC is full of stuff I've written—so much stuff that I don't remember writing some of it. Once I've written a story, I feel attached to it, and over-sensitive to criticism of it, for a little while—but then I let it go. Some of the old stories get rewritten or cannibalized for new projects and others are just forgotten. And all of them end up part of my huge pile of "stuff". My guess is that most writers regard their stuff in a similar way.

People who have written one short story don't feel this way. That short story is their first child. If you tell them it's a deformed mutant, or if you just look at it without smiling, you're asking for trouble. In my defence, your honour, I didn't know it was his only story.

Oblivious to the gathering storm clouds, I carried on. I wrote two more drafts. Some of his suggested "improvements" bothered me, but I ignored the nagging feeling. This was a *collaboration* so I couldn't expect to have things my way all the time. But when it comes to the basic craft of writing, you really should trust your gut feelings.

As you practise your craft as a writer, you learn that you have to leave room for the reader's imagination to fill some things in. You make suggestions in order to evoke their own memories and experiences in a way that creates a movie in their mind's eye. You also present clues that allow them to draw their own conclusions. In short, you "show don't tell". Also, reader and writer enter into a pact that means the reader will suspend their disbelief and simply accept some of the crazy ideas the writer wants to present. You don't have to—and shouldn't—explain everything. In this story-world, some things just *are*. The notes I was getting from my collaborator said that I should explain things more because readers might not "get it". And he was concerned that I was making some parts of the story funny...

I did explain to him at this point that I wrote in a particular style—and that plot and humour were important to me and my "brand". As someone who made a living as a writer, I could only put my name on something that I felt would meet my readers' expectations.

I also made the mistake of sharing some notes on story structure. Just a summary. I'd spent twenty years or so learning and practising this stuff.

I was still too self-involved to see the storm approaching. I was writing a novel and doing edits on a non-fiction book and doing this "fun" collaboration on the side. But I was aware that the water was getting a bit... choppy.

I realized that my collaborator regarded this novella as his second child. It was no longer a story we were just knocking out for fun in our spare time—this was *the* story. Part of his legacy. Perhaps he regarded it this way all along and I hadn't realized. I tried to tackle this by suggesting that we take a break and spitball a few ideas for short stories. My logic was that if he was involved in creating more than one story, he wouldn't be so fixated on the Second Child.

I referred to the story structure notes I'd shared—and was accused of imposing "rules" that shouldn't apply to creative endeavours. They restricted an artist's freedom, he insisted. That was the point when I noticed the dark clouds and the flashes of lightning. But I still wasn't smart enough to change my ways. I wrote first drafts of three or four short stories based on ideas we'd talked about.

He, meanwhile, was still nurturing his second child. And he said I was an idiot for not liking Ingmar Bergman movies. He thought our story—*the* story—should be more like a Bergman movie. I think the term Scandi-noir was used.

At some point, I'm not sure when, his notes stopped being about what was wrong with the story and started being about what he thought was wrong with me. I brushed off the first few comments—he was an old friend and he was entitled to have his opinion about me. Some of what he said about me was right but some of it was way off base—offensively so. Bear in mind that we still hadn't been in the same room for maybe a decade or so.

He did a complete rewrite of our "Second Child of the Maltese Falcon" novella. And by *complete*, I mean literally. Every word I had written was changed. The only thing left of mine was a couple of lines of description in the first paragraph. I'm not used to being rewritten. As a writer I have been edited. And censored. And I've had pieces I've written pulled from a planned publication. But I have never had something I've created completely obliterated. Writers don't do that to each other.

I thought at first that he'd done it deliberately to try and teach me a lesson. Perhaps he wanted to show me how he'd felt when I "took it upon myself" to write that first draft on my own. I didn't recognize this new version. The dialogue was "on the nose"—and there were pages of it explaining things that didn't, in my view, need to be explained. And the basic structure of the plot—set-up, rising action, crisis, climax, and resolution—was gone. And so was all the dark humour. This parrot was deceased.

I thought about writing a carefully considered critique, but in the end said, "Fuck it." I told him there was nothing of mine in this draft and nothing in it I liked. I was happy for him to take my name off it and he could take it as his own and do whatever he liked with it. I didn't tell him what I thought he should do with it.

If I was writing this as a story, I'd say things ended there. I learned my lesson and moved on—battered by the storm but wiser for the experience. But I didn't. We started a new project. I encouraged him to write the first draft—I had learned *something* at least. It was more Ingmar Bergman than Raymond Chandler. I did make some suggestions to try and introduce a semblance of plot, but they weren't received well and if I'm honest, my heart wasn't really in it. That project also withered and died—at least from my point of view. I suppose that he ended up with two new children that sort of resembled Ingmar Bergman, meaning his pile of "stuff" was now three times the size it had been.

There are also a handful of short stories that I wrote during this that are actually pretty good, but they'll never get beyond the first draft because I don't *own* them. Dividing up the property is always tricky after a divorce. Think how awful it must be if two collaborators were actually married!

At this point I should insert the moral of the story—but all I can say is "Writer beware!" Don't make the same mistakes I did.

CONTINUE YOUR COLLABORATION JOURNEY

Eager to keep filling that brain jar with knowledge coins about collaboration?

Co-Writing A Book
Collaboration and Co-Creation for Authors

In this collaboration mini-course, bestselling authors J. Thorn and Joanna Penn share tips on **how to successfully co-write a book (both fiction and non-fiction)** and avoid the pitfalls along the way.

To find out more, visit: https://creative-penn-courses.teachable. com/p/co-writing-a-book

*

Collaborations: When the Whole Is Greater than the Sum of the Parts by Craig Martelle

Craig Martelle brings the experience of dozens of collaborations to this book, outlined in an easy-to-digest format that covers all the collaborating bases.

Download your copy: https://books2read.com/u/3LD79N

OTHER TITLES BY DANIEL WILLCOCKS

The Rot Series (with Luke Kondor)

They Rot (Book 1)

They Remain (Book 2)

They Ruin (coming soon)

Keep My Bones

The Caitlin Chronicles (with Michael Anderle)

(1) Dawn of Chaos

(2) Into the Fire

(3) Hunting the Broken

(4) The City Revolts

(5) Chasing the Cure

Other Works

Twisted: A Collection of Dark Tales

Lazarus: Enter the Deadspace

The Mark of the Damned

Sins of Smoke

Keep up-to-date at

www.danielwillcocks.com

CPSIA information can be obtained
at www.ICGtesting.com
Printed in the USA
LVHW040359200620
658459LV00008B/1251

9 798644 262946